Ghosts Believe in Me

By
Rick McCallum
Founder of the Hollywood Ghost Hunters

© Copyright 2020 - Rick McCallum

All Rights Reserved.

ISBN:

No part of this book may be reproduced or transmitted in any form or by any means; graphic, electronic, or mechanical, including photocopying, recording, taping or by any information storage retrieval system without written permission of the author.

Printed in the United States of America

Dedication

This book is dedicated to all of the wonderful people who have been a part of my life, to all my family and friends, and to my cousin Joyce Larson who was always kind to my mom, and who still puts flowers on my mom and our grandmother's grave.

This book is also dedicated to those brave ghost hunters who even if they are alone still "Dance in the Dark"

Foreward

Rick McCallum's paranormal experiences from childhood on have been amazing and continue to this day. As he shares some of his history in this book I believe readers will be surprised to realize many early experiences are actually a family history.

The hauntings I've read thus far would be considered extreme by most yet as a whole this family just coped, adjusted and moved on. I believe this is why Rick is one of the most adventurous paranormal investigators I've ever known.

Rick founded Hollywood Ghost Hunters after years of working as a SAG actor, a stuntman and as a stunt coordinator with his friend Kane Hodder after they had a shared experience while filming at the Ohio State Penitentiary. Rick has been fortunate enough to investigate many places, any one of which would be on most people's bucket list. He shares many of them here in his book. This book is an excellent read with just enough moments that give you pause when you consider following along in the steps of a Hollywood Ghost Hunter. And yes. Ghosts DO know him.

Rick will tell you his one single superpower is that people are nice to him. I would disagree. As you come to know him through this book, or if you've been fortunate enough to spend any time with him, you will know that his one superpower is compassion. He will still think it stems from you.   Kat Hobson

My friend Kat Hobson is the voice of Fate Magazine Radio, the owner of WBHM digital radio, and Paranormal Experienced Radio and I am very proud to have her write the Foreword! ... Rick

Table of Contents

Chapter 1: Introducing…Me..13

Chapter 2: Was this my first psychic experience?..................................21

Chapter 3: The most haunted house in America...................................27

Chapter 4: Real Angels on Earth..41

Chapter 5: Is that you?..45

Chapter 6: When it comes to women, I am the dumbest man in America.........47

Chapter 7: The Voice...49

Chapter 8: Darkwolf … The Movie..55

Chapter 9: Waverly Sanatorium..61

Chapter 10: Classic prank at Mansfield Prison......................................67

Chapter 11: Teaming up with Ghost Adventues...................................69

Chapter 12: My mom and I had an awesome bond..............................75

Chapter 13: My first Scotland trip...81

Chapter 14: Premier Paranormal Tours..89

Chapter 15: The nicest ladies in all of Scotland!...................................97

Chapte 16: Even I can't believe it!...101

Chapter 17: Frozen by a hellish growl… in broad daylight!................105

Chapter 18: Spirit on a Bicycle in Brentwood, Tennessee...................109

Chapter 19: The sword..117

Chapter 20: The Queen Mary..121

Chapter 21: Kane Hodder interview..125

Chapter 22: Sometimes I just can't help myself!.................................131

Chapter 23: Project Metalbeast..133

Chapter 24: The Oman House..139

Chapter 25: Sometimes there is so much more to find.......................147

Chapter 26: The Graber Olive House, Home and Family TV Halloween Ghost Hunt...151

Chapter 27: The Pioneer Saloon...155

Chapter 28: The Buffalo Central Terminal..161

Chapter 29: Rosslyn Forest, Scotland..165

Chapter 30: Hunting with Scottish Paranormal...................................171

Chapter 31: Balgonie Castle..175

Chapter 32: The Real Mary King's Close..181

Chapter 33: Colonel Allensworth State Park..187

Chapter 34: England is extraordinarily haunted..................................195

Chapter 35 The Hellfire Club, and Leap Castle....................................203

Short Stories

Bachelor's Grove..24

Our Paranormal roommate...51

Sometimes Kane Hodder gets a little extreme......................................78

This still makes me wonder..107

The Bedroom Battle...111

On the set with the Hollywood Ghost Hunters...................................112

Strange things at the William Heath Davis House..............................113

The Little Girl in the Window..119

Have some of the strangest things happen..137

Me at work..138

Scarefest!...144

The Strange case of Donna...192

My Only Superpower

The first thing you need to know about me is that I have a superpower. I only have one superpower, and the stories within this book should prove it in spades. My only superpower is that people are really nice to me. I know that sounds funny, but I have people I barely know do things that absolutely astound me. I don't have any idea why, but I am certainly glad that I have it; I hope I deserve it, and that it keeps up for as long as I stay on the top side of the grass.

I have been able to have awesome friends and family, and I have gotten to do and see way more than my share of wonderful locations. Many of them being while working on a movie (Kane Hodder brought me to Australia to work on the film Charlie's Farm, as well as many other places I wouldn't have gotten to see). I have done many dangerous things while in the stunt business; I've put some in here as well.

Chris Sun, Director, me, Kane and Nathan Jones on the set of Charlie's Farm

At the age of thirteen I developed a passion for ghost hunting, or maybe it just came naturally, for I have seen and felt things my whole life. It apparently ran in the family, my dad and I had some incredible things happen at his house in Texas while I was there when I was just out of college; those things are detailed in the book.

My mom, became very ill with cancer and I had gone back to Chicago from Los Angeles in early 2013 to take care of her, and I never had to do anything more grueling, physically and mentally, but I think in the last week of her life she finally realized how much I loved her, and the night she passed away, I was holding her hand when she crossed over. It was a torturous four months; I was a physical wreck from having to do everything to help her. I was so sleep deprived one of the nurses who would check in on her took my blood pressure and told me I was on the verge of having a stroke. I smiled at her, and said can we pencil that in for later, I need to take care of my mom. It was the hardest thing I have ever done, and I wouldn't trade one second of it. She had been diagnosed with Stage 4 lung cancer fifteen years earlier; no one ever dreamed she would fight the good fight for so long. Even her doctor called her a walking miracle.

It was during this time that I was sitting in the living room with her one night when she said, "Oh, my Indian is back." Wait! What Indian?!

My mom slept in a recliner for many years, and she could see all the way to the back door from her chair. She told me that every once in a while she would see him inside the backdoor, and that he would stand quietly there and watch her. I asked her why she had never told me, and she said I know he is here to watch over me. I was barely into processing what she had said, when she looked at me and said quietly "I have seen spirits my whole life"... The strange part, well, OK, it is all strange, is that my dad and mom had been divorced since I was around ten, and hadn't seen or talked to each other since, but both had many experiences with the paranormal. I guess it is pretty obvious where I got it from. There will be other stories about my mom later in the book, as well as my dad.

If you find the timeline a bit confusing, it is because when I was young we moved an incredible amount of times; my dad was always trying new things and going to new places. It is only when I went to live with my mom that I had some stability in my life living in Chicago from about thirteen until I graduated from college. I bounced around a lot myself after college, living in Texas, California, Colorado, back to California, then to Tennessee. Sometimes it is hard for me to remember where I was. If it seems like I am in different places at the same time, that is not the case, the reason it may seem that way is that this is not a day by day story of my life, just things that I hope you will find interesting, and I was all over the country at various times.

I hope you enjoy the stories; they are for the most parts in chronological order. I've added other people's ideas of what may have happened on our hunt, I believe it is always good to have other voices chime in, to get other people's versions of what happened, or to provide validations. I hope some stories will scare you, and that some will make you laugh, that you will enjoy the journey through some very famous ghost hunting locations… and that I can share the many strange and wonderful things that have happened to me… I have had a few experiences that were so extreme that no matter how I write them they won't seem real, but they are 100% factual, and even I have to admit, they are hard to believe, but I guarantee that everything in here is as accurate as possible.

Chapter 1
Introducing…, me...

At the age of three, my mom and dad took me to a John Wayne movie, where the key scene was a stage coach going over a cliff. Obviously very impressed by what I saw, I drove my little red pedal car as fast as I could through our living room past my parents, who watched in horror as I headed toward the flight of stairs directly in front of me. My dad tried to catch up but could only watch as I went airborne, and then I, while still in the pedal car, rolled end over end, crashing into the floor at the bottom of the stairs. I received two black eyes for my effort...

At the age of twelve, when I lived in the country, a small place called Sam's Valley in southern Oregon, my dad was having a bunch of people over for an outdoor barbecue. Deciding that the party needed a little excitement, I rode my Honda 50 motorcycle through the party, all while I was standing on the seat. After the party, I received a sore behind for my effort. I entered the stunt business in 1982...who would have guessed?

I moved back to Chicago to live with my mom when I was thirteen, we lived on the South Side, or as I like to say, the Best Side. My high school years were very wet, because I was a member of the swim team, and I was a lifeguard in the summer. Still more water in my life as I became a certified scuba diver, one of the youngest in the U.S at the time.

After graduation from high school I wanted to join the Navy. I really wanted to see if I could become a Navy Seal. I know I had the skill in the water, but looking back I am very glad my mom convinced me to go to college.

During the summer break at college I had many different jobs. I was a garbage man; I worked as an overseer for my district in the CETA program, and made extra money as a basketball referee. It was during this time that I realized that I just wasn't cut out for a regular 9 to 5 job; my wanderlust was a little too strong.

I had always wanted to do something physical, and for many years had been fascinated by the stunts I saw in movies. I really wanted to give that a try. I didn't have much money, and absolutely no contacts in the film business, but I knew where they made the movies. I packed up my clothes and headed to Los Angeles.

My first movie was Lone Wolf McQuade, a Chuck Norris movie that was filmed in El Paso.

While working on the movie I met another stuntman by the name of Kane Hodder, who became one of my best friends, and we have worked in numerous movies and TV shows together. Kane went onto to play the character Jason Voorhees in four Friday the 13th movies, as well as Victor Crowley in all four Hatchet movies...

With the help of Kane, Director Richard Friedman, (Darkwolf, Born, among many others, which Richard had me as stunt coordinator) and Director Adam Green of the Hatchet series, who cast me as John, the silent hunter in Hatchet 2, and has had me on several other projects, including Saber, which won Best Picture and Best Action at Comic

Con, I have gone on to be in more than 75 movies and TV shows.. Thanks guys!

While filming a movie at Mansfield prison in Ohio, a very haunted place, me and Kane were walking through the back cells of the prison when we saw the shadow of a man cross in front of us about 30 yards ahead ..Kane took off after it, but it vanished. Now I had been ghost hunting since age 13, and then living in a very haunted house in Texas in 1979, and Kane had ghost hunted around the island where he grew up, and neither one knew the other was interested in ghosts.

That night the Hollywood Ghost Hunters was formed, along with several others in the horror movies, including Ra Mihailoff, who played Leatherface in the Texas Chainsaw Massacre 3...

The Hollywood Ghost Hunters were featured on the hit TV show Ghost Adventures, and became good friends with Zak Bagans, Nick Groff, and Aaron Goodwin, all who are the real deal when it comes to both ghost hunting and being good guys, and we hope to hunt with them again, it was a heckuva good time...

The Dream that Defines Me

The dream started when I was around five years old. It was extraordinarily vivid; I would wake up knowing that I had just lived through something that was very real to me.

In this dream I was in a place that I would say was like old time Rome or Jerusalem, and there was a group of people all in a giant circle. I could hear the sound of swords clanging together as there was an epic battle going on in the middle of the circle. I couldn't see what was going on but being so little I wiggled my way through the crowd till I could get to the front.

Being just a kid I was confused by what I was seeing, as all the people were dressed in very old time clothing, the kind of clothing that you see in shows about Jesus' lifetime, the white linen with the rope belt and things like that. As I got closer to the front the most awesome sight came into view, as I saw what appeared to be monsters, what I now know would be considered demons, and standing there was a man totally encircled by these demons, who took turns attacking him. A titanic fight was ensuing, the man fought ferociously, and even as skilled and brave as he was, I could see he was tiring and it was just a matter of time till the overwhelming size of the demon army would kill him, and even being a child I was very confused, why weren't the other humans helping him? The Warrior was fighting furiously with a demon in front of him when another snuck up behind him, the Warrior turned quickly and killed the one behind him who immediately dropped its sword and fell to the ground, and the Warrior turned and faced the other demon and was fighting him. .... I decided I needed to help him, and just as I started to move out the man turned around and mouthed the word" no" at me. I went in anyway and picked up the sword and went back-to-back with the Warrior. A demon advanced on me and being 5 years old lifting the sword was almost impossible when suddenly the sword was light in my hand! I was suddenly full grown, strong as a man, much more capable, and I killed the demon with one swipe. I turned back and saw the face of the Warrior, who for some reason I knew was an angel. He smiled and turned back to engage with another demon that was attacking him. We fought furiously for a long time, felling demons right and left, it seemed there was no end to how many there were.

I felt a sharp pain in my side and could feel myself falling. I would always jerk wide awake right then. I continued to have this recurring dream for years and I always struggled to understand the meaning behind it. It finally dawned on me that I was being asked to make a choice between good and evil and that I had chosen good. I have always found comfort in that dream now that I know what it meant. I told my dream to my friend Cait Fair who drew this picture which I truly treasure.

My Grandpa's Last Ride (and my first paranormal experience)

It had been a very difficult day, my mom and I were riding on a train from Chicago to Paducah, Kentucky to bury my Grandfather, and it was a very long, somber, emotional trip knowing that we were taking our last ride with him.

We arrived at the station and as my Grandpa's casket was taken from the train to the funeral home for the burial the following day. My mom and I made our way to the closest hotel near the cemetery.

We were on a tight budget, and the hotel was old and kind of worn out. I was thirteen years old at the time and as we checked into the hotel the clerk apologized and said they only had one room left, and my mom said we would take it. The clerk politely told my mom most people wouldn't stay in that room because it was haunted.

My ears perked up when I heard the word haunted, and thought this might take our minds off of the upcoming funeral. And hey, I was thirteen and they said we would be staying in a haunted room, I felt like I had been given a Golden Ticket to Disneyland!

The clerk smiled as he gave us the key, and he looked at me and said "good luck", and all of a sudden I wasn't sure about staying there, but up we went to the room on the second floor and my mom opened the door. I have never seen a hotel room like this before, it almost looked like a volleyball court with wooden floors and two beds on opposite walls about 15 feet apart, a few chairs and a table. It was not the Hilton for sure, and there was a neon light outside the window that added to the creepy atmosphere of the room.

It was to be an early day for us tomorrow, so we jumped in our beds and with all the stress and travel I fell right to sleep. And then it happened, the experience that would start me on this fascinating, frustrating and always exciting paranormal journey...

I had been asleep for several hours when I heard my mom yell... I sat up to see her bed rolling across the floor towards me, and then I felt my bed start rolling towards her... they picked up speed and collided into each other in the middle of the room. We just sat there looking at each other for a minute, and she said "I guess the clerk was right".

We figured that maybe the floor was bowed, but I got a glass, laid it on its side and set it by where the beds were, and it wouldn't roll on its own, even if I gave it a good push. We thought maybe a truck went by and the vibration caused the beds to start rolling, so we pushed the beds back and shoved them towards the middle, and shoving them as hard as we could they only went about three feet. No matter what we tried, rolling coins, a glass, nothing would roll on their own.

I was hooked from that day on, and have ghost hunted in Australia, Switzerland, Ireland, and Scotland for weeks at a time, and also England, which is ridiculously haunted. I have hunted many of the most haunted places in America, and many times I have done them alone. It has been quite a while since that first night, and I have been touched, growled at five different times (other people also heard them).

I also believe a few spirits tried to attach to me in Goodsprings, Nevada; the voice saying "release him" as I turned to leave was a definite clue... I have seen a man get knocked out at an Abbey in England, heard a howl in the forest very late at night around Rosslyn Chapel in Scotland, and so many more it's hard to even know where to start...

But I think the very best place to start would be at the beginning...

Chapter 2
Was This My First Psychic Experience?

When I lived In Sam's Valley Oregon with my dad, I was about 13 at the time, just before I went to Chicago to live with my mom.

I was super excited because my dad was taking me hunting. I really didn't want to shoot any animals, but I really wanted to shoot the rifle and spend the day with my dad, something that almost never happened. My dad never seemed to have much time for me, so this was something special.

We walked up Table Rock Mountain looking for deer, but didn't see any; I don't think my dad would have shot them anyway, it wasn't really his style.

We shot the rifle at different things as we walked, and I had a real good time with my dad, as he showed me how to shoot, and how to load the gun. It turned out I had a natural eye for shooting, even my very hard to impress father was impressed.

After a long walk back down the mountain we came to the front door, where my dad showed me how to make sure the rifle was empty, he checked the chamber a second time, and certain it was unloaded we went inside.

We went up the stairs to the kitchen to grab some lunch when my stepmother Gay set upon us, screaming at my dad for bringing a rifle into the house when there was a baby. My little brother Cash was still less than a year old. My father told her he had doubled checked the rifle to make sure it was unloaded, but she started screaming at him and wouldn't stop. He lost his temper and took the rifle, slid the bolt back and slammed it home, and being incredibly angry, took the barrel of the rifle and jammed the end into his right eye just under the brow.

I saw him put his finger around the trigger... I don't know if it was my imagination or my subconscious but I heard the word "no" scream inside my head, and I grabbed the barrel and pulled as hard as I could. The gun fired... The bullet went past my father's forehead and hit a dark brown ceiling beam, which was about eight inches thick, and tore a hole up into the roof. Gay grabbed Cash and my stepsister, screaming hysterically all the time, and ran out the door and didn't come back for a week.

My dad went into his bedroom and closed the door, leaving me alone and staring at the hole in the ceiling. He never said a word to me about it... but I did save a life...

I also saved another life right after that, and I only am telling it because it is so cool...

There was a lake about 150 yards in front of our house, and my dad and some other fathers had built a wooden raft with a high dive on it, and we would play on that raft all day, some of my favorite childhood memories... until this happened..

Cash's mom Gay decided to swim out to the raft while she was holding Cash, who was about a year and a half old... It was about thirty yards to the raft, and Gay was a very good swimmer, she could make it to the raft easily...

There were two dogs, Major and Baron, who were half Great Dane and half German shepherd. They weighed roughly 60 or 70 pounds each, big hairy monster dogs.

Ghosts Believe in Me

The dogs wanted to swim to the raft and play, but they weren't very good swimmers and began to founder and began to panic.

I was watching as the dogs went for the nearest floating object to save themselves, unfortunately, that was Gay and Cash. The dogs started trying to use them as a raft and their paws were smacking the heck out of Gay and Cash, forcing them underwater.

Gay was putting up a tremendous fight, trying to fight off the dogs, whose paws were clawing at her in desperation, and she only had one hand to try and fend them off and to swim with.

I ran to the edge of the raft to jump in and help them, but suddenly one of the dogs knocked Cash from her grasp. He sunk under the water, while Gay was screaming for him and still trying to get the terrified dogs off of her.

I was already at the edge of the raft and dove in, trying to figure out the right area to find him. I was swimming under water as fast as I could, actually probably even faster than I could because I didn't want Cash to drown.

Now it is hard to say what happened next without a big smile on my face. I had picked the right angle to find him; he was about twelve feet down, sitting on the bottom! He was sitting there as calm as could be, I'll never forget the sight as he came into view.

All he was wearing was white shorts, it might have been a diaper, and he had his legs out in front of him.

I am absolutely flying towards him when he looks up and sees me coming. I'll never forget how he raised his arms up towards me like he wanted to be picked up, and his tiny fingers were pointing at me and he started opening and closing his hands like he always did when he wanted to play.

I was still worried he might drown, so I grabbed him and shoved of the bottom as hard as I could. When we surfaced Gay had gotten away from the dogs and was looking for him when we popped up. When she saw Cash I don't think I've ever seen a happier person in my life!

I have to tell you I love telling this story because Cash was the coolest little dude ever, he just took it in stride, never cried, you couldn't even tell he'd been in serious trouble. He was the most chilled out one and a half year old ever!

BTW, if all this saving lives keeps up, I'm going to need a cape!

I have gone back to that house twice to see if the hole was still there, but both times the people were on vacation. It was an 800 mile drive, so I guess I still have something that needs closure there.

I frequently wonder where the screaming "no" in my head came from. Was it psychic? Was it precognition? Or was it just a scared kid trying to save his dad?

I guess that was what the two trips were about. But after all the years, I guess I'll never know...

Bachelor's Grove 1975

I have been intrigued by the paranormal since I was just a kid, and my interest has grown every year, and I have been lucky enough to experience some very interesting things.

Ghosts Believe in Me

I've been touched, pushed, growled at in Waverly Hills, Linda Vista Hospital, the William Heath Davis House, even in my own home (all with witnesses), and I've heard voices that called out my name when no one else is around, so I could, and probably will tell those great ghost hunting stories in the future. This story, however, regards one of the best instantaneous pranks of all time, when it comes to ghost hunting. By instantaneous I mean we didn't plan it, the circumstances at hand left us no choice.

Back when I was in college in Chicago, Bachelor's Grove was the paranormal must see place, and always wanting to check out any haunted place, my roommate, Jerry Clemens, also known as Psycho, a nickname he richly deserved, another friend named Scott and I all headed over there.

I saw the episode on Ghost Adventures about Bachelor's Grove, and you probably did too, but the place was much different in 1975 when this happened. There was a long gravel road, about 200 yards long, tree branches overhung the road, the kind of place every horror movie should be made.

After going down the road your senses were already on edge, just from how creepy the place looked. And when you got to the cemetery, a bunch of the graves had sunken in about eighteen inches; there was a pond next to it which really made it scarier than hell...

In 1975, the place was off limits, you could get arrested for being in there, so people would park far away and sneak down the road. You didn't want to drive down it, because if you drove in and the police came, you couldn't get out, the only way out was back in the direction you came from, as the road dead ended by the cemetery.

Three of us had just walked into the cemetery when a car came creeping down the road, we didn't hear it coming till it was only about fifty yards away. We were positive it was the police, and there was absolutely nowhere for us to run, the road the car was on blocked one way, the pond blocked another, and there was a fence and all overgrown trees you couldn't get through on the other sides.. What to do?

I looked quickly around, then told Psycho and Scott to lay flat in the graves that had sunken in, so if the cops shone their flashlights across the cemetery, we would be a little below ground and they wouldn't be able to see us. We laid there very still and quiet, desperately hoping not to get arrested, when we heard car door close and a girls voice say " I don't want to go in there", and then a guy's voice say " don't worry, I'll protect you". We heard other people whispering, a girl giggles, so we knew it wasn't the cops.

I had an inspiration while I was laying there, two actually, the first being that arms were going to shoot up next to me and drag me underground to my demise, and second, these people came here to be scared, so let's make that happen! I whispered to the other guys, we were in three graves in row, and said, "When I count three, sit up and turn and look at them"

I waited until they were very close, and then counted... On three, we sat up in unison, turned and looked at them...

That was in 1975, and judging by the way they screamed and ran, I'm not sure if they stopped yet...

Chapter 3
The Most Haunted House in America

My room in our house in Chicago was extremely small, so much so that laying on the bed I could stretch out and put my feet on one wall and my hands on the other, and could stand up and reach the other two walls, it was a toy room for my cousins when they lived there.

I am a tall guy and I need a pillow to wrap my arms around when I sleep, and my mom was going to the swap meet so I asked if she could get me one. For some reason, I will never know why, she got me a small round red satin pillow, which is definitely not my style, but I was grateful she got it for me and it turned out to be a pretty good hugging pillow, it just looked really strange on my bed.

My friend Tom had helped me move my dresser and had made fun of my pillow, it was very out of place in my room...

It wasn't long until the visits started... I would bolt wide awake absolutely positive someone was standing next to me, neither my mom or Gram would come into my room at night, but as sure as anything I've ever felt, I knew without question there was a presence that was standing next to me. I didn't budge, sure that if I moved he would kill me, why else would someone be looking at me in that tiny room?

The feeling would fade away, leaving me confused and full of questions. It happened several more times, each one as intense as the first.

Heading to Texas

It was around this time that my dad called, which was very surprising because we hadn't been on the best of terms and hadn't talked for at least a year. We talked some things through, and then he invited down to Texas for a visit, and I decided I would go. I got my friend Tom to go with me, it was a long drive from Chicago and having some company would be good for sure. I told Tom about the night time visitor, about how terrifying and absolutely positive I was that someone was in my room, and we couldn't figure it out.

We stopped in Memphis for the night, and the next morning we went to Elvis's house because I am a big fan of The King. We headed down the road after that, and arrived at my dad's house around 10 PM. My life would never be the same after that night.

My dad let us into the house, introductions were made, there was a man named Wally also there, who worked for my father. They had been at a local bar celebrating Wally's birthday, and had to take him back to his car. I told my dad I was dead dog tired from all the driving, and was going to bed. He pointed out a room, and the rest of them went back to the bar, leaving me alone in the house.

I went into the room, a small bedroom with a canopy bed, a window letting the moonlight shine in towards the foot of the bed. I closed the door behind me, there was one of those sliding locks on the door, and so I locked that, and lay down on the bed, very tired. I wasn't in bed for but a few minutes, when I heard what can only be described as a loud exhaling of breath, more than loud enough for me to sit up and look around. I could see the room clearly from the light coming in through the window at the foot of the bed... there was nothing there, so I lay back down. Again, a little louder this time, I heard the breath. My first thought was that the air conditioner had turned off; andI was hearing the sound it makes when it turns off. I was wrong... It happened again. Air conditioners don't turn off twice, so that wasn't it.

I thought that maybe my dad had a dog, and maybe he was under the bed, so I got up and looked all through the room, under the bed, and in the closet... Nothing... Once again I got back into bed, this time I was sitting up so I could see the room, and truthfully, fully aware that something was wrong... My senses were on alert; I could feel something in the room, but still couldn't see anything... Then it happened, a defining moment in my life, the moment that led me to a lifelong obsession with the paranormal.

I was sitting up in the bed , looking forward, when a very loud breath , a breath that was unmistakably meant to scare me, it was so close to me that I could actually feel the force and heat of it on my neck right behind my right ear. I jumped out of bed, grabbed the door, but it wouldn't open because of the slider lock... I yanked that door so hard that I broke the frame and the slider lock in my haste to get out of that room.

I didn't even want to be in the house, so I went outside and stood on the front lawn. After a few minutes my dad turned the corner, he lived at the end of the cull de sac, and pulled into the driveway. He and Tom got out and walked toward me, they could both see something was wrong.

My dad looked at me for a minute, then laughed and said "he got you, didn't he"? I asked him what he meant, and he let out a loud exhale... I looked at him; I couldn't believe what he had just said... I said "you knew about this"? He just smiled and said "it happens all the time".

My roommate from college Jerry Clemens came to visit several months later; this is his experience in the house...

> Every night while lying in bed, a WHOOSH of wind came thru the room. No windows or doors were open. It Continues

There was an amazing thing that was about to be revealed. As my dad, Tom and I were sitting around talking, my dad told me he thought about me often, and had felt bad about us not talking for so long and many times he would dream that he was standing in my bedroom looking down at me as I slept.

Tom looked over at me with a curious look on his face, I am sure my face had a stunned expression as I suddenly knew who the night time visitor was!

I knew that I couldn't take this on face value so I asked my dad what bedroom looked like. My dad had never been to my house, and I had never spoken to him about my room.

He shocked me when the first thing he said was he didn't even see how I could fit in the room because my bed took up almost the whole room. I asked him if there was anything else about the room. His answer? A small round red satin pillow... I have never had that feeling again... Hmmm, I guess the paranormal runs in the family...

Pay Attention!

Later that night, Tom, my dad and I were in the living room, talking about ghosts. My dad asked me what I thought ghosts were, and I told him that I had heard that they were energy from a dead person. I had barely said that, when a flash, like the flash from an old time flash bulb went off in between us.. What had I gotten myself into? I became a committed ghost hunter that night, and in the couple of months that I was there, that house proved to be by far the most haunted house I've ever been in, and it's not even close... I have at least a dozen stories I could share, most of them when somebody else was with me that would knock your socks off.

Face to Face With a Giant

My dad's house in Fort Worth Texas had a big backyard that was fenced, and we had had a Great Dane as I was growing up, so I asked him if we could get one. He said sure, find out how much they cost, so I started looking around. There was only one place anywhere near us that had Great Dane's and it was a lady who raised them to be show dogs. I explained that I wanted to get a Great Dane and she said their price started at $500. Now this was a 1979 and that was a pretty significant amount of money, so I told my dad how much they wanted and he said "Ah the heck with it let's go look."

I called the lady and made an appointment and my dad and I jumped in the car and drove about 30 miles to her kennel. We introduced ourselves and she started bringing dogs out for us to look at, but all these dogs were show dogs, all beautiful in their own right but not what I was looking for, I wanted a dog that would play with me and wrestle and do all the kind of things that dogs do.

We must have looked at 20 dogs when she finally said well that's pretty much all I have, and when she said pretty much, that said to me that there was another dog somewhere. I asked her about that and she said all she had left was one huge dog who had a little bit of an under bite, hated people and he was vicious. I really didn't care that he had under bite, so I asked her to bring him out. She was really wary about bringing him out and once again told us that he hated people and was vicious. I asked one more time and she said OK and came back with this magnificent looking animal that was wearing a muzzle.

She came up about 8 feet away from us and had him sit, and I looked into his eyes and I didn't see vicious at all, to be truthful, it seemed he looked back and I felt an instant connection with him.

I asked her to take the muzzle off. She refused at first, but I knelt down across from the dog and was even with his face and I told her take the muzzle off, and if he bites me it's on me and I won't hold her responsible. She thought about it for a minute, told me I was making a big mistake and said OK.

She removed the muzzle and I was face-to-face with this giant dog looking him in the eye, and I said to him quietly "Come here." The dog looked at me but didn't move. For some reason I really wanted this dog and wasn't ready to give up on him, so I patted my chest and said "come here". What happened next will stick with me for the rest of my life, as the dog walked right up to me and our faces were maybe 6 inches apart. I smiled at him and as God is my witness he stepped forward and rested his head on my shoulder.

The lady stood there with an astonished look on her face as I rubbed the big dogs' ears and back of his neck, I stood up and told him to sit, which he did instantly.

I told the lady that I would really like to have him and she said OK, so I asked her how much she wanted for him. She looked at me with huge smile and said I have never seen anything like this in my entire life and I've been around dogs forever.

She then told me that she thought the dog whose name was Tubby would never find a home as he had never interacted with anybody in a good way, and she always feared she would have to put him down…

She looked at me and she says I don't know what just happened there, but he is yours and I'm not going to charge you.

We loaded Tubby into the car and he leaned on me pretty much the rest of the way home. That dog and I had an unreal bond and he didn't have a vicious bone in his body… And then the unexplainable happened…

I Think He is Going to Try and Kill Me

I've already told you about my first night stay at my dad's house, when I got a terrified by something that happened in the bedroom. It got worse after that.

One day I was sitting cross legged on the floor watching TV. Tubby was lying near me sleeping. And he was one of the sweetest dogs you would ever find in your life. He took a big liking me so we palled around a lot and he was rarely very far from my side.

All of a sudden his head snapped up and his face instantly changed, his ears went back, his eyes narrowed and his teeth bared, a growl came from deep inside him. He looked like a tiger before it attacks.

I had never seen him, or any other dog, have a look like that in my life. I was very sure he was about to attack me, but I knew that dog loved me and would never hurt me, but he was in full attack mode, and started to rise, stopping in a crouch like he was preparing to jump, he actually was quivering, his body shaking with what I could only describe as rage. I tried calming him; I was not in the best position to slug it out with a giant dog, as I was only about four feet away sitting on the floor, I was talking quietly to him, saying "it's me Tubby, its ok". He didn't seem to hear me, his eyes were locked on me like a laser beam, and I kept saying" it's ok Tubby, it's me". It was then that I realized he wasn't looking at me at all, but he was looking at SOMETHING BEHIND ME!

I knew if this gentle animal was acting like this, he was seeing something or someone, and there was no one in the house besides me. I instantly thought there was burglar and yelled "get 'em!" Tubby went by me in a blur as I rolled to my feet to help him... What I saw still makes me wonder... Tubby was in full attack mode biting at the air, and actually jumping on his hind legs, biting, growling, and his paws were flailing at the air... There was no one there. Tubby stopped and stood listening, and then he turned towards me.

The old Tubby was coming back as he calmed down, whatever he had seen had gone... I'll never forget that day, or the feeling of my friend fighting who knows what to protect me. We would soon learn what was in the house...

Don't Challenge the Spirits!

I was still staying at my dad's house when I met a friend of his who was staying there as well. He was a 6'2" 350 pound bearded man who was an artist. He had been a bodyguard, wrestler, just a huge guy. We quickly became friends. My brother and I were in my dad's bedroom when Giovanni challenged me to a wrestling match. He charged me and I ducked under him, grabbed him, lifted him and spun him around and we both landed on my dad's bed, with me on top. All we heard was a very loud crunch as the metal frame of the bed flattened to the floor. I guess that they don't make anything like they used to. I mean come on, it broke from having two dainty little guys like me and Giovanni crash landing on the bed and that flattened it?! Sheesh, we only weighed a combined 580 pounds!

Giovanni was an artist who worked in powdered metals and resin, combining them and then pouring them into molds. After the metals and resin would dry he would pull them from the molds and rub them with OO steel wool to make the metals appear... They were very high class artwork, his technique allowed him to inlay many different colors and patterns of metals, and when buffed were extraordinary.

My dad let Giovanni set up his shop in his garage, where I had my heavy bag and speed bag so we would frequently be in the garage at the same time, me working out and him working on his metal sculptures.... As a lot of his sculptures had lead and resin together he would always wear very long over the elbow yellow industrial gloves to protect his hands. We were talking one day about the house being haunted. Being very skeptical he said the whole idea of spirits was bullshit and told the ghosts to touch him, all the while provoking them by calling them names, saying they couldn't do anything to a person because they didn't exist, and even if they did they didn't scare him one bit.

I was hitting the speed bag when all of a sudden I heard a very loud slap sound and heard Giovanni yell! I spun around to see what was wrong and I saw a big red hand print on the side of his face.

He started screaming at me saying that I had hit him, when he realized I was standing about 20' away and couldn't possibly have hit him and got all the way back to the speed bag.

At first I thought he had done it to himself as a joke, but judging by how red the side of his face was I didn't think he did it when it suddenly dawned me that he was wearing his gloves that were covered in powdered lead and the lead would have been all over his face if he had done it to himself.

I believe Giovanni lost his skepticism that day and realized it's really not a good idea to provoke a spirit too much. He was much more interested in the paranormal after that!

The Garage Remained a Hot Spot

My dad's house was laid out like an H, his bedroom and garage on one side of the house, the living room, and dining rooms and the kitchen in the middle, and my bedroom and his office on the other end. The garage and my dad's office both were next to the backyard, the bedrooms at the front of the house.

My dad and Vandy were in his room, I was in mine, and Cash was sleeping on the couch. Very late one night, we had gone to bed hours earlier, I woke up to the sound of someone hitting the heavy bag in the garage. I figured it was Cash and I didn't want him to wake my father, who I knew would be royally pissed off and I didn't want Cash to get in trouble. I got out of bed and was surprised to find Cash walking towards me with a strange look on his face, when he said was "I think someone is in the garage"

Of course all my warning signals went off, the Great Dane was in the backyard and as we started to walk quietly toward the garage door my dad's door opened and my dad and Vandy stepped out, my dad holding a pistol.

OK, that answered one question, it was none of us in the garage, no other people were staying at the house, and the only answer was intruders… We made a plan that I would go into the backyard and me and the dog would come into the garage from the outside entrance while my dad and Cash would go into the door across from his bedroom… We knew they were still in there because we could hear the punches hitting the heavy bag. I slipped outside and Tubby came to my side, he could hear the sounds as well. I heard my dad open the door and I rushed in with Tubby right behind me... My dad and Cash, with Vandy right behind them came flying into the room. There was no way they could have gotten out, my dad at the entrance and me at the only other door, and the overhead doors were closed and locked.. My dad turned on the lights and the heavy bag, which probably weighed at least fifty pounds was swinging back and forth like a metronome from the chain attached to the ceiling. What happened next was a sight I'll never forget…

We made sure no one was hiding in the garage, and we all knew about Giovanni getting slapped in the face, so we were on edge while we tried to figure out exactly what the hell was going on. A long, deep growl came from next to me, I looked and Tubby was staring at the bag. As the bag was swinging back and forth it suddenly sounded like a punch hit it and the bag flew backwards, and as it flew back it only got halfway when we heard the sound of another punch and the bag flew backwards again!

My dad got angry and told them to knock it off and the punch sounds stopped. Tubby was still very much on edge, alert. We stood and talked about what we had just seen, it was hard to believe but we had long been convinced that if this house wasn't the most haunted house in America it would certainly rank up there with anything you could find! As they say on every late night commercial, "But wait, there's more"!

We turned to leave going through the door towards my dad's room, I was last in line because I had let Tubby out into the backyard through the other door, and as I had just closed the door on my way out, right behind me no farther than three feet the speed bag attached to the wall went flying from another punch, the sound echoing through the entire garage!

We all stood in the hallway when my dad just shrugged his shoulders and said "what are you going to do"? And then he headed into his bedroom, and as he closed the door he said quietly to me "let the dog in the house"...

> Of course, one could hear the speed bag on a daily basis and although you didn't see anyone or anything close to the speed bag, you could see the movement of the bag. You could see them (or rather shadows) on the deck as they left every evening about the same time – 3 shadows making their way across the deck and up the hill. Vandy Richards

The Chase

My younger brother Cash had moved into the house, he was about 13 at the time, and we told him of the house being haunted, which he didn't believe at all. He does now! Let me explain... My dad, Vandy and I had all told him of the things that went on in the house, and he was positive we were teasing him, so I told him how the spirits had turned out the light in my bedroom one night when I asked them to.

He said if the ghosts listen to you, have them get me! He gave me a playful whack on the back of the head and took off, with me in hot pursuit. Playing along with him, as he started to run through the dining room I yelled "get him ghosts"! Just as he rounded the table and headed for the kitchen the spare dining room chair that was against the wall flew sideways about two feet and landed on its side directly in his path to the kitchen.. Cash was looking back at me and running and when he saw the chair falling in front of him he hit it and went flying head first into the kitchen and landed face down sprawled on the floor, right near Vandy who was cooking... she saw the entire thing, and Cash rolled over and started yelling, totally freaked out, "they really listen to you"!

In time, we were all involved in so many things that it was hard to remember all of them... And Cash and I ended up looking for them together...

> Another Arlington house incident (there were so many)... I was in the kitchen and we were getting ready to make lunch. The house was laid out so that there was a wall that divided the kitchen from the dining room and the den. One could walk in a circle and go into all the rooms. Cash, Rick's younger brother was being silly and running a circle into all the rooms and although we had asked him to stop – he was still running. Rick asked him to stop running or he would ask the ghosts to stop him, of course, he just kept running. As he was making another circle – he was in the dining room heading to the kitchen when a chair flew in front of him and he fell over it. We had to laugh as the ghosts finally got him to stop. Vandy

I Get the Scare of My Life

Living in a house as haunted as the house in Texas could make you feel a little apprehensive as you would walk around at night locking up and turning out the lights. My dad's office was directly across from my bedroom, and I walked into his office to turn off the lights. His office had two floor to ceiling windows about a foot and a half wide; one on each side of the back wall, on the other side of the wall was the backyard, which would usually let in a good amount of moonlight, giving the room kind of a creepy, horror movie vibe.

    I was looking towards the window to the backyard when I turned the light off, and what I saw made me jump backwards and smash into the wall! What I saw was a head with what looked like horns looking in the window! It scared the hell out of me! I flipped on the light and was very happy to see Tubby looking in the window, his ears pointing straight up the way they do on Great Danes… I was still catching my breath when I turned out the light and as I started to leave the office, directly behind me I heard a very deep ominous laugh inside the room behind me… I went outside and had Tubby sleep in my room… that was a very long time ago and thinking about that laugh still sends shivers up my spine…

Chapter 4
Real Angels on Earth

There have been many times in my life where I've been in a pretty tough situation, and it was only through luck and kind people that I managed to get where I needed to go...

Back in the mid 1980's when I was trying to gain some footing in the movie business, I would jump into my beat up old 73 El Camino and go between California and Chicago, sometimes Denver, and it was on one of these excursions that I was coming from Chicago heading to Los Angeles that I ran into a bit of trouble. To say I wasn't financially above board back then would be putting it mildly, I often only had a $100 to get from Chicago to Los Angeles, and very late one night in Utah I got a flat. My spare tire had gone flat, and I had nothing to put on as far as another tire. My only option was to ride on the rim about 2 miles to a gas station I could see way off in the distance. I pulled into the gas station and a young guy came out, and I told him I needed a tire. He asked me why I hadn't put the spare on and I told him I didn't have one, so he said "then you really need two tires, right"?

The young guy looked at my rim and told me that from driving on it I had ruined it, and it was unusable.

I still had about 700 miles to drive and very little money on me, and I told the attendant that... He stood there for a couple of minutes thinking, and said "I think I can help you out, follow me" and he led me to the garage area out back. He said that he had just changed the tires on his car, and he thought his spare would fit my car. He looked around and came out with a tire that looked almost brand new, it also had a rim and he said how much can you afford. I told him I had exactly $60 to my name and I had to drive 700 more miles, he turned around walked back and came out with the mate to his other tire that also had a rim on it.

Drive your car in here he told me, so I went and got it and we put it on the lift and he changed both of my front tires and said now you can use that other tire I took off as your spare and you have a matching set on the front. I told him I honestly don't have enough money to pay for this and he said the tires, the rims, the labor, everything, I'm only going to charge you $25 total. Now I know that that young guy who is working in the middle of night at a gas station was giving me tires and rims that were worth about 200 bucks. And he didn't look like he had a lot of money to his name either, so I realized that I had come across an exceptional human being.

I told him there was no way I could possibly thank him for his kindness, and he just told me people had been kind to him. He started to lower the lift and suddenly said "shit!"

Just then a man came in who had driven up to get gas. He joined us as I asked the attendant what was wrong and he said by driving on the rim I had destroyed all of my lug nuts and he didn't have any in the shop to put on my car so it wouldn't be drivable without having the lug nuts. Now it was extremely cold out, maybe around twenty degrees, and it was looking like I was going to have to put on extra clothes and sleep in the back of the El Camino which was not only very uncomfortable, but also extremely dangerous. I had slept in the car one other time and got so cold that when I woke up I barely made it out of the car into a truck stop, my entire body was shaking, it was very hard to walk, I almost fell several times and I had to really will myself to make it. Lesson learned.

The man who had just come in told me to come with him, and he went out and took one lug nut off of each of his tires and handed them to me.

I told him I couldn't believe that someone would do that, he told me he just wanted to make sure I got home safe.

Now that happened over 30 years ago, and I think of those two guys very often, and I like to think that I've passed on that humanity whenever possible due to the great lessons they taught me… I really wish I had gotten their names and phone numbers. Maybe there would have been a time when I could have helped them, but the more I think about it, I don't think I was supposed to remain in contact with them, I prefer to think of them as real Angels on Earth.

Ok, Now Where Did That Come From?

I was working on a movie in Australia named Charlie's Farm, and the accomadations we stayed at were absolutely devoid of any creature comforts… my room had no TV, radio, telephone, desk, chair or closet. It was a beautiful area that was used for retreats for Boy Scouts and the like, so the grounds were awesome, but the rooms had no maid service of any kind, so no one ever entered my room except me. I went down to the dining hall and grabbed a plastic chair so I could have something to sit on while I would read a book… there was nothing else to do, but the other crew was also staying there, and they were awesome people. Every morning I would take a long hot shower. I would go get dressed and then sit on my chair to put on my shoes and socks. Every day for weeks I sat in the same place, looking towards the bathroom. This appeared the mirror as I was looking into the bathroom..

A woman's handprint.. I put mine next to it, it is obviously not mine, mine is much bigger.. I never saw that on any of the days before, and I would have, but this formed while I was looking at the mirror… Remember, no one else ever came into the room…

…Ghosts Believe in Me

Chapter 5
Is That You?

Back in 1985 I was a big fan of the game show Sale of the Century, and would play along every day. One day my brother stopped by to play basketball with me, but I made him wait until the show was over. He asked why I was watching and I said I'm going to go on that show and kick some serious ass… He said you'll never do it… Game on!

I went to an open audition for the show, and roughly 300 people showed up. They had us stand in front of the crowd and talk about ourselves to see how we would react, and being used to being in front of people I didn't have a problem. A bunch of people were let go after that, and then we moved on to a 50 question test that I was fortunate enough to get 46 answers right. They cut the crowd down to roughly 25 people. They said they wanted us to come to the office to play a test game.

My interview was to be in about a week, so I made sure to play the game every day it was on TV.

I arrived at the office and we launched into a series of games, and I noticed they were putting some contestant's pictures off to the side.

After we had all finished the contest coordinator said she would read off the names of people who had been selected to appear on the show. I watched carefully as the photo pile dwindled down to one, and I was the last one chosen. I said to the coordinator as I was leaving that I barely made it by the skin of my teeth. She smiled and said that my picture was on the bottom of the pile because that was the first one picked to be on the show, which made feel pretty good about my chances.

I was on for four days, I won the first three days, lost on the fourth day, and I didn't win anywhere near what they are showing in the picture.

I did have a very interesting thing happen while we were filming the show however. The talent coordinator took all the contestants outside so we could all watch a Bob Hope Special being filmed. We watched for about ten minutes and then filming was over. Bob Hope and a man walking with him started to walk away, and he was smiling and waving to us when he sees me at the back of the group. He suddenly comes through the crowd, he grabs my hand shakes it and says "I haven't seen you in a long time, how have you been?"

I say I've been great, and he turns back through the crowd and heads out.

All of the other contestants are really impressed that Bob Hope is a friend of mine, but the truth be known, I had never met him before, and I just figured he was playing to the crowd and he chose me because I was in the back. I was wrong.

Several years later I was walking into my bank just as Bob Hope was leaving the counter. He saw me and walks over and says it's great to see me again. We chatted for a couple of minutes; he was an extraordinarily nice man. He then said goodbye and went on his way.

I always wonder who he thought I was. I hope it was someone cool.

Chapter 6
When it comes to Women, I am the Dumbest Man in America

I will freely admit that when it comes to the ladies, I am as dumb as a post. If a girl gave me a Cadillac, and a kidney, I'd still wonder if she liked me. I got a great object lesson while working on a movie; it came in the form of one of the moms whose young son was working on a movie I was doing stunts on.

My friend Rick Rosenthal was the studio teacher who was in charge of teaching the kids, including her son. When her son was filming, she, her name was Ann, Rick and me would hang out and watch the scene. We had a great time, we all became friends, and one day at lunch, one of the extras, a pretty girl dressed like a nurse walked up to me and said hi and me being the polite type (ok, stop laughing!) I said hello back. It seemed like the gentlemanly thing to do. She was very sweet, and we talked off to the side for a while... They called for the extras to come back to the set, she said goodbye, stood and looked at me for a minute, and then headed off. Ann came up to me and Rick, who had just walked up, and asked me if I had gotten the girls phone number. I asked why she would give me her number, and she said "man, you are right, you really are stupid when it comes to women, that girl was flirting her little heart out." I said, "No, she was just being nice."

I thought about it for a few minutes then told her she was right, and that I was such a dope I'd need someone to kick me in the shin to get my attention.

The next day a different extra, also dressed like a nurse came up and started talking to me, it's not like I'm all that, people meet and talk on the set all the time, there is really nothing else to do.

We sat down and had lunch together, she told me she wanted to be an actress, and was doing work as an extra to get some experience. She asked me what I was doing on the film, so I told her I was the stunt coordinator. She seemed really interested in stunts, so I told her about some of the things we were going to do on the film, and she was very excited about seeing them.

They called for the extras to return to set, so we stood up as she would have to head out.

Rick and the mom are watching, and the mom walks over to us, tells the girl excuse me, eases her back a couple of feet and then kicks me right in the shin! The nurse quickly left, afraid of why some woman was kicking me, and I heard hysterical laughter, so I looked over and Rick Rosenthal was about doubled over he was laughing so hard, and so was Ann!

I had to admit, that was pretty dang funny! Painful, but funny…

Chapter 7
The Voice

Many years ago I was back in Nashville Tennessee at my dad's house watching the family business, he and his wife Vandy had gone to Australia for a month for a vacation.

I had driven my 280ZX back to Nashville and planned on selling it as I had bought another car.

I decided that it would be nice seeing as how I had already put an ad in the paper that I would change the oil for whoever bought the car. I went down into the garage and jacked up the car and got an oil pan and ratchet to unscrew the oil plug.

The house where my dad and Vandy lived was in a very upper scale neighborhood; the houses were not that close to each other, it was a very quiet area, especially at night.

My dad's house was on a hill, and to put your car into the garage you had to drive down a hill into the garage, so it was very isolated from the surrounding houses.

I crawled under the car; a 280ZX is a very low slung sports car so that even with the car on the jack there wasn't much room underneath. I got the plastic oil bucket; they are designed low to the ground so they will fit under the car, then put the ratchet on the oil plug and started trying to loosen it.

It wouldn't budge. I kept trying, and was starting to get frustrated, and more determined to get that plug off.

I started putting some serious muscle into it and could actually feel the car move side to side a little, but the plug still wouldn't budge.

By this time I was very mad, and was getting ready to put everything I had into getting that bolt off. I put the ratchet on the plug again, made sure it was on good and solid, then took a deep breath and was just starting to yank as hard as I could when I was startled by a voice... it said very clearly "let it go."

I instantly thought someone was in the house! I scrambled out, and went through the house... nothing, nobody... I went back into the garage and opened the roll up door and looked outside to see if anyone was outside, sometimes people would walk their dogs down the street in front of the house... again, no one was around. It was about 11 at night, so the neighborhood was very quiet.

I closed the door and stood by the car, confused by the voice, then decided it was probably my imagination because I couldn't get the plug off.

I crawled back under the car even more determined to finish the job. I put the ratchet on the plug and again I heard the voice! "LET IT GO!"

This time it wasn't a suggestion, the voice was full of authority, demanding I pay attention, it was no doubt commanding, much louder than the first time, and I instantly felt the urgency and importance of the voice.

I quickly slid out from under the car, and I had barely cleared it when the car fell off the jack!

It came so close I actually felt the door brush the hair on the top of my head!

I realized I had been saved by the unseen, I no doubt would have been crushed by the car, and if it didn't kill me instantly I would have been caught under the car until someone came to find me, and with both my dad and Vandy in Australia on vacation no one even knew I was there.

I don't know my Guardian Angel's name, but you can bet I am a believer, and you can also bet he got the biggest thank you my trembling body could muster!

Our Paranormal Roommate...

Many years ago, my girlfriend and I had a studio apartment in one of the trendier apartment complexes. The backlot of Universal Studios was across the street, and Warner Bros. studios were at the bottom of the hill, so a lot of entertainment people lived there.

We had tennis courts, basketball courts, pools and hot tubs, sand volleyball, so there was lot to do. I had gone out to play basketball, and Lauren had stayed behind to read a book. I had been playing about a half hour when I saw her come quickly into the basketball court. At first I thought she had decided to play, she was a very good player, but as soon as she got closer, I could immediately tell that something was wrong...

I was lying on the bed in our studio apartment, reading a book I'd gotten from the library entitled True Ghost Stories of England. My cat, George was curled up next to me. I remember feeling just a little bit anxious as I read through the tales of hauntings in the dark, old histories of English villages. Some months earlier, Rick had mentioned that he thought we had a "presence" in the apartment, something he'd felt and even seen in the bathroom mirror as a kind of light. I didn't take it too seriously, but not because I didn't believe in ghosts. I just hadn't seen or felt anything myself and, as Rick said, whatever it was didn't feel evil or mean, just present.

Earlier that evening he had gone out to play basketball and I was supposed to go with him but I had my new book and I was looking forward to some quiet time alone to read. Suddenly George raised his head and looked toward the kitchen, which in our tiny apartment was only a few feet away. There was nothing moving, no noise that I could detect, but then George jumped off the bed and went into the kitchen and stood looking up to a specific spot above him, as if he were looking at someone standing at the sink.

He looked so intent that I chuckled and jokingly said "Are you looking at our resident ghost? If so, there are cookies on the counter if it wants one." At that moment, all the dishes in the dish rack sitting next to the sink crashed into the sink and George ran away and hid behind the bed.

I jumped up and went over to the kitchen and looked at the dishes that had been sitting on the rack moments before and the overwhelming feeling I had then was to get the hell outta there. Now. I hurriedly put on my sneakers, grabbed my keys, told George I'd be back soon and ran out the door. I stood in the hallway outside the apartment and inserted the key to lock the deadbolt

As I did so I heard behind me a kind of chuff, like someone who was breathing hard after climbing stairs and I thought "Oh good, Rick's back." I turned, expecting him to round the corner to our little alcove. No one was there. I was alone in the hallway. I felt adrenaline flood thru me and I took off running down the hall, down the stairs and out of the building. I kept running until I reached the basketball court and, after letting myself in the gate, I plopped down by the fence and took a few deep breaths to slow my breathing.

> I must have looked pretty freaked out because Rick saw me and left the game to come ask me what was wrong. I told him about George and the dishes and sound of someone breathing behind me. I also said I didn't think I wanted to go back to the apartment anytime soon, except to get George. He just smiled and said "Now do you believe me?"
>
> Lauren Peterson

We lived in that apartment for quite a while, and while I would see shadows and movements from time to time, and George the cat would suddenly start staring at something, but we had no other big occurrences.

Chapter 8
Darkwolf… The Movie

It is very rare when you get to work on a movie with two of your very best friends, but with Richard Friedman directing, and Kane Hodder, who is playing the human half of Darkwolf, and I am playing the werewolf half, we are all together on a dark night at a warehouse downtown. It is very cool that Kane and I are playing the same character, just different halves...

Steven Williams about to get killed by Darkwolf

We are getting ready to shoot a very dangerous stunt, so here I am all dressed up in a werewolf costume getting ready to jump on the hood of a car, and it peels out going in reverse, and as I am trying not to fall off the car, I start breaking the windows and smashing away at the roof… and that is dangerous enough, but nothing like what comes next..

We need a little backstory here, while I will be doing the physically dangerous part of the stunt, the hardest part is the actual driving of the car, going in reverse with the actors in the car, then hitting the brakes so the car goes ninety degrees, in effect cracking the whip and launching me off the hood. I hired one of the legends of the stunt business, none better at doing car stunts, Chuck Waters... OK, that is three friends on the movie! I trusted Chuck to hit his mark so I would hit the right spot for the camera.

Richard wanted a big crash so Chuck and I grabbed a bunch of steel 55 gallon drums, and a couple hard plastic ones to make a wall of drums, roughly six feet high, and two barrels wide. If you haven't ever moved one of those drums, they are really heavy. So I have to not only hit the right camera spot while I am flying through the air, I am going to be hitting steel drums!

You can always tell on a movie when a stunt is dangerous, because a lot of the cast and crew will come out to watch. One of the actresses came up to me and said "are you going to get hurt?" (I thought it was very cool that she was worried about me)... I just smiled and said "I'll let you know in just a couple of minutes.

The Makeup Special Effects guy was Robert Pendergraft, who I had just met, but would become not only a friend, but a very active member of our ghost hunting group... Yep, that is four friends!

Ghosts Believe in Me

He was putting on the headpiece of the werewolf, I actually would look out a screen in the neck to be able to see, making sure it was on good and tight, we wouldn't want my werewolf head flying off and ruining the scene! (John Buechler was also working on the movie, number five!)

I was walking towards the car when I saw off to the side my friend and Hollywood Ghost Hunter member Louis Horowitz standing there. He was to be in the movie in his very first acting job, but that his scene wasn't for a few days, so I thought it was pretty cool he came out to watch... Bingo! Six friends!

I walk to the car, climb up and signal to Richard and Chuck that I am ready. Richard yells "ACTION", and Chuck peels out and off we go!

I am watching the barrels coming up when Chuck hits the wheels and brakes, sending the car into a perfect reverse 90 degree slide, much like cracking a whip, I feel the momentum heading towards the barrels, I see the mark where I want to hit the barrels, and using the momentum Chuck just gave me I launch myself shoulder first into the barrels, hitting my mark exactly! (I told you Chuck Waters is the best driver around!)

Here is when the fun starts, first off hitting the barrels felt like hitting a steel wall, I went into them and they started flying around like bowling pins, hitting me from different directions, I hit one and was tossed like a rag doll in a half circle, and I was trying to figure out where I was in the air when the weight of them hitting me kept knocking me in different directions. The edge of the last barrel hit me in the side of the head, and I went and landed on my lower back right on the edge of one of the barrels that was sitting upright... I had absolutely no idea where my crash pad was, it was on the other side of the barrels, but fortunately I landed perfectly, and then rolled off camera so they couldn't see me as the car sped off.

I had barely hit the ground when Robert Pendergraft came up and asked me if I was all right, in truth I had my bell rung a bit, and they told me to lie still while they took the headpiece off. When it came off there was blood coming out of my left ear, they were worried that it was something really bad, but I knew it was from the edge of the barrel hitting me in the ear.

I asked Robert to look at it, and he could see the cut in my ear. Richard looked down at me and said are you ok… I looked up smiling and said" just say those three little words I really want to hear".

Richard looked confused and said "what three little words?" I just laughed and said, "Perfect, moving on". Richard just laughed and hollered out "perfect, moving on", which for those who don't know movie lingo, it means they liked the shot, everything is great, and on to the next scene, and best of all, you don't have to do the stunt again!

Robert helped me up, and I couldn't help but feel pretty good by all the people watching who came over to see if I was all right, many said they had never seen anybody hit anything so hard in their lives! Perfect thing to say to the stunt guy!

You would think that was by far the most dangerous thing that happened while filming, but you would be wrong. We were filming a scene where the Darkwolf corners two people in an industrial elevator, the kind that has the doors that you slide up manually.

The Darkwolf (me) was to hit the slide up doors three times, each time as hard as I could, with the elevator going up. I hit it hard, crouched down, and launched into it again, really hitting it hard. When I hit it the second time the headpiece moved forward blocking my vision.

Ghosts Believe in Me

I knew where I was so I crouched again and just as I started to really hit the safety screen of the elevator I heard someone scream "stop!", and then I was very forcefully pulled backwards.

I stood up and adjusted the headpiece so I could see, and almost fell over at what I was seeing. I had hit the elevator so hard that the safety screen had gotten stuck into the elevator door, and it went up with the elevator.

I stood there totally quiet for a minute as I looked at the empty space that I had almost launched myself into, and down the empty elevator shaft where I would have fallen, it would have certainly injured me very badly or worse.

I turned to see who had screamed and grabbed me and saved me. I saw Robert Pendergraft standing there, the Special Effects Make up man, who just smiled and said "that was way too close". It is a very good thing Robert is a huge guy, about 6'5" and nearly 300 pounds and stopped me just as I started to ram into the elevator.

That was many years ago and Robert and I have done many more movies and ghost hunts together. Thank you doesn't seem like enough, but I'll say it anyway… Thanks Robert!

Chapter 9
Waverly Sanatorium

My family and I had produced trade shows, exhibit shows and thrill shows for over 40 years and we had three of the largest Home Decorating and Remodeling shows in the country. I had just finished one in Nashville when Kane called. Kane told me he had gotten us access to Waverley Sanatorium for a ghost hunt.

I was more than excited as Waverley Sanatorium is one of the icons of the ghost hunting world. I couldn't wait to get there! As I drove up the long drive up on to the Hill and saw this gigantic building I knew I was in for something special. I met up with Kane and the rest of the group and we figured out what we are going to do for that night. I also met Tina and her husband

Waiting for us at the location were other HGH members Chris Carnel, Barry Blaisdell, and Steve Nappe, who had come with Kane. I was fortunate enough to have Tina Mattingly who is the owner of

Waverly Sanatorium to show me and the group with me through the entire building so that we could find out the hotspots that we wanted to ghost hunt.

We all took turns going to different locations among those being the fifth floor where the spirit of the nurse touches people and had hung herself there, and then the death tunnel which is extremely awesome in every regard.

We all took off and went to different floors, and Barry Blaisdell, a girl who was a guest and myself headed out to the Body Chute.

The death tunnel is probably close to a 100 yards long and very steep downhill. As we are making our way through the tunnel trying to communicate I noticed the girl was looking around as if she was hearing something. I watched her closely because I also was hearing something. I finally asked her if she was hearing anything, and she said yes she was. I asked her what she was hearing. Every ghost hunter knows you don't say what you heard because it can give someone a suggestion and they might not be sure of what they heard, so they almost always agree with you when you do that. I always ask them what they heard, because I already know what I heard.

She told me what she was hearing what sounded like very light singing. I told her I heard the same thing but what I heard was more like a Gregorian chant, or the chant that they do when they're following the hearses in the New Orleans funeral procession. Barry said that he also heard it so we headed back up the ramp so I could see if there was anybody up above that could be making the sound or playing music from their car. As we got up there a car was pulling up so I asked him if he had been playing any music and he said no, and then I asked him if he saw anybody else outside and again he said no. It was time for us to change locations so my group went up to the fifth floor.

As we are walking in to Room 512 I felt somebody caress my right forearm very gently. I thought it was the girl with us, but she wasn't close enough to have done it. I told them that I had just felt something caresses my right forearm and she said that is fantastic! I wish I could get touched. She stopped right in mid-sentence. I asked her what was wrong, she had a strange look on her face, and she says somebody just touched my face!

Evidently the stories of the nurse touching people inside 512 have some validity. As we were walking back out into the hallway one of the weirdest things that has ever happened to me occurred. The girl said she saw a shadow figure go into the Room down the Hall from us so I took off after it. I went into the Room and it's probably 10' by 12' with just a chair and maybe one box in the entire room, hardly anything in there at all. As I was standing there all of a sudden I heard a very deep growl that sounded like a watch dog or a guard dog. I looked slowly around, not wanting to get bit, that is how real it sounded! There was no dog in that room; there was nothing in that room but me. As I turned around I saw Barry and the girl standing there and I asked them if they had heard the sound. Both shook their heads, the look on their faces told the whole story.

> While investigating the Waverly Hills Sanatorium, in Louisville, KY, Rick, myself, and another investigator were about to enter room 502. As Rick entered the doorway there was this very loud, yet distinct, low growl. At first I thought we had encountered a

> stray dog, but it quickly became very clear that we were the only physical entities there. Rick slowly turned around and asked "Did you guys hear that?" All we could do was nod in agreement and continue the investigation. There were other strange occurrences throughout the night but that one stood out for sure.
>
> Barry Blaisdell

Paranormal occurrences were far from done, as Kane had asked Tina and the other members which was the most haunted place in the building not including the death tunnel, because that's where everybody thinks it is, but he wanted to know where the people who work there all the time thought it was. We got a very surprising answer when they said it was the front lobby. Tina was nice enough to let us be the first people to investigate that area.

Kane came up with a great idea; we would each go in and sit inside in the dark by ourselves with no flashlights for 15 minutes each... I can tell you that is was like being in a sensory deprivation tank, everything was so dark and quiet. I have to say that sitting in a well-known haunted location in those conditions will definitely heighten your senses, knowing something could be right next to you and you couldn't see it, because as part of the experience no flashlights were allowed. We all took turns in there, Kane went first, and after 15 minutes were up, I went next, and then Chris Carnel went, then Steve Nappe, and then Barry Blaisdell.

When we all had taken a turn we started talking about what we had experienced. Kane told of how he could hear what sounded like leather soled shoes walking right towards him, and when I listened back to the voice recorder they are there as clear as can be. It is also clear they walked up to only a few feet away from Kane!

Ghosts Believe in Me

While I was in there I heard what sounded like furniture being moved, I also heard footsteps and the door rattle behind me. Kane also said had said that he had heard the door rattle. Now some of you may not know who Chris Carnel is but he played the Miner in my Bloody Valentine part 3-D and I've seen him roll over cars at 70 miles an hour as a stunt man, so it's not like he's easily scared. I asked him how it was and he said he had never been more scared in his life. I was shocked that this was coming from Chris, so I asked him what had happened. He said that he heard the door rattling and then he heard someone walk up behind him, and as he was sitting there very still he says he heard what sounded like a sword being pulled out of the scabbard! He was the only one who heard that.

Steve Nappe had similar experiences, while it was quiet for Barry...

The sheer size of Waverly sanatorium is completely impressive; it is gigantic in every way. When my group got up on to the top floor and we were walking we kept seeing what looked like shapes of people, not actual people but dark shadow shapes of people popping in-and-out near the doors. It only happened a couple of times but we all had seen them at the same time, so that was very interesting.

Just from my remembrances of hearing the singing in the death chute, hearing everything that happened in the lobby, getting touched in Room 512 and then having something growl at me in the Room next to 512 made for a fantastic ghost hunt. Thank you Tina Mattingly for inviting our group, it was a blast!

Chapter 10
Classic prank at Mansfield Prison

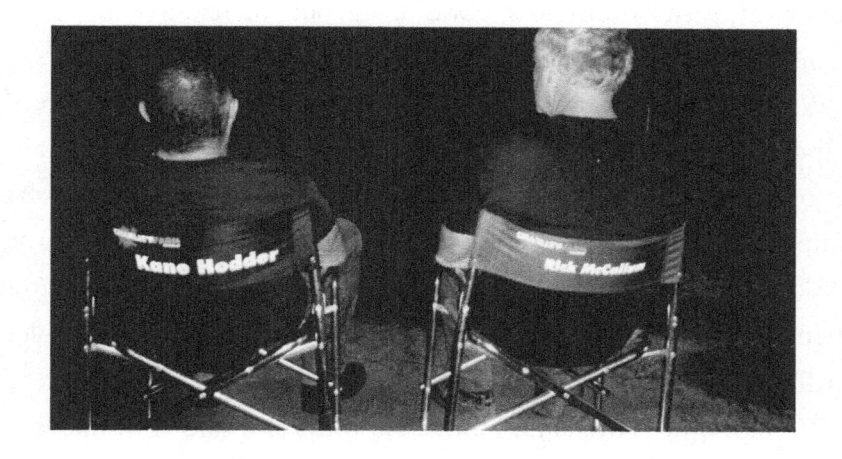

First, a word of caution, if you ever see this on a movie set, and you are the shy or timid type, or don't like pranks or guys with a bizarre sense of humor, you might want to look for a good place to hide...

Most of you know Kane, R.a. and I were doing a movie called Fallen Angels at the prison, and that is where The Hollywood Ghost Hunters was formed, but this isn't about that, it's about leaving me and Kane alone in a very dark, very scary prison...

One of the actors on the set, Myron St. John, also is the guy who ran the Mansfield Prison Halloween Haunted House, and when he said all the stuff was stored there, we went looking for it! Kane and I found the stash of bodies, and all the scary stuff that goes with it.

We found a very creepy looking mannequin, it looked kind of like Angus Scrimm, and we snuck it onto the set. There was a small, winding walkway that went from the front area where the movie base camp was, out through the cell block. Everybody had to go through it to get to the cell blocks, where the actual filming was being done. It was a very creepy looking area.

We found the perfect place, just as you made a small turn there was a doorway, with a room no one was using, but you had to pass right by, no matter if you were going to or leaving the set.

We set the mannequin inside the door, close enough to see the shape, but you would have to lean into the room to see the detail of the mannequin. We quickly set it up and headed back towards base camp. We had gone maybe fifty yards when Kane asks me "do you think anyone will see it? " The words were barely out of his mouth when we heard a girl let loose with one of the highest pitched, blood curdling screams I've ever heard!

We kept on walking, and I looked at Kane and said "I think we can take that as a yes"…

Chapter 11
Teaming up with Ghost Adventures

Most of you probably first heard of The Hollywood Ghost Hunters from our teaming up with Zak Bagans, Aaron Goodwin and Nick Groff on their hit TV show. When Kane called and said we were invited to be on the show, and what did I think, my answer was a resounding "hell yes!"

Rick, Zak Bagans and Aaron Goodwin

The shoot we did was actually a two day shoot, because we did the interviews in a prop warehouse, the skeletons and bloody animals, the creepy furniture gave our interviews the horror movie vibe, which looked pretty cool on TV.

One of my favorite parts of the day was when Kane grabbed Zak in a chokehold! It was really a great chance to get to know the guys, and to a person they were all cool, including Billy Tolley, who was more behind the scenes back then.

The next day we all met up at the Pico House, the building that would be our haunted lockdown location for the night. We all toured the building and the basement, which was actually in the building across from us, but they were both connected as far as the hauntings went.

The story of the Pico House is of a race riot between the Chinese Tong, the Mexicans (these were people that had been in the area when Pio Pico was Governor, I believe the area had been part of Mexico at one time) and the white people, due to the Tong murdering an Irish cop.

There were 19 people killed in the riot, right outside the doors of the Pico House. It definitely seemed like a place that should have some pretty good activity!

We grabbed our equipment, we didn't need much, and the GA guys had tons of it. Zak led us to the basement to get the hunt started. We had barely walked in when Nick Groff and I felt a very strong energy that we had just walked through, it was funny because we walked through it, then immediately turned around and asked if each other had felt it. The camera shot a close up of Nick's and my forearms, and you can see the hair sticking up, and the goosebumps on both our arms.

While we were down there we heard footsteps, and I heard footsteps above, if you watch the show you will see me pointing at the ceiling pointing it out to Zak. As we walked back into the other building Aaron noticed a door open on the second floor, the door had earlier been closed, it seemed like something wanted us to go up there.

Zak led us up to the second floor where we tried to draw the spirits out, Kane tried, Zak was trying to get a reaction, as the story was a security guard got kicked very hard in the back, ran out and never came back. R.a. asked the spirit to kick him, actually asked twice but no luck… it seemed like the spirits didn't want to show themselves… until…

The group started heading to a different part of the building, but I decided to watch the door that had opened by itself. Nothing happened with the door, but as I started to go out the door, I spotted two very discernible shapes walking one after the other going from right to left… We were on the second floor, and the shapes were on the walkway of the second floor directly across from me.

I hollered out what I had just seen, and we tried to debunk it by having everybody do the same thing they were doing when I saw the shapes, including walking in the same places and directions as I watched. It definitely wasn't our guys because they had all gone to the left of me, and from where they were couldn't have cast shadows going along the wall that far to the right, and then continue to the left.

Excellent! The place is starting to come alive!

We all split up. Zak and R.a. teamed up, Kane and Aaron went down to the underground area to try to capture some voices on the recorder. Nick and I went to the basement across the street, where we had felt the energy earlier, hopeful of finding it again. I can only relay what happened to me and Nick; I had to wait till the end to see what experiences the others had.

We walked to the end of the long hallway, where Nick set his gear bag, and we had barely gotten there when we heard loud footsteps above us, walking down the hallway on the floor that was above us.

We followed the sound, walking right below it, we knew our guys were in the other building, and that the security had made sure both buildings were empty, so that anything we heard would not be from other people, well, not any that were alive, anyway…

As we got to the front of the hallway that was at the front of the building, we started hearing voices from the other end! Nick and I hurried to the other end, and it turned out that it was Nick's Spirit Box, which was surprising because it been turned off. Could it have gotten turned on by bumping into something in his bag, sure, but either way it was spitting out words?

Just then we heard loud noises coming from the other end, where we had just come from! And they were unmistakable, they were very loud footsteps, some above, and some that sounded like they were on our floor! I turned to Nick and asked him if he thought something was messing with us, drawing us from one end to the other? He agreed that sounds were too loud to be random, and the way the sounds would get louder on the other end of the hallway.

Walking back to check on the Spirit Box, which we could hear it going as we got near, we had barely stopped to listen when we heard very loud noises, much louder than before coming from the front end. When we got to the end of the hallway, we were both sure that what it sounded like was someone running and stomping on steel stairs. At the end of the hallway the left hallway was blocked off, so we went farther and were surprised to find the stairs were made of concrete, while we were positive it sounded like steel steps.

We heard loud knocking from the side door, and checking it found it was Zak and a security guard coming to get us to join the other guys and to see what Billy Tolley may have found on the voice recorders. I asked them if they had been pounding on the front door, trying to figure out what made the steel sound. Zak and the guard both said no. It was very strange, but I would find out what it was… about a year later.

When we got upstairs, Kane, R.a., Aaron and Billy Tolley were all around a long table with Billy setting up the audio that had been captured on his computer. The clear cut winners in the EVP race were Aaron and Kane; Kane had actually gone into one of the small brick underground rooms, Aaron on the outside with a camera shooting into the room. Aaron made a crack about getting killed down there, and Kane said "you're filming me, I have an alibi!" We were shocked when Billy played the next part…Immediately after Kane says he has an alibi, two different voices were caught, both with Hispanic accents… The first voice says "anything good?" and then the second voice says "don't say anything, they don't know nothing!" Even Kane was impressed, and that is not easy to do.

A girl named Layla Halfhill, who is editor of the website www.scarepop.com, and who had seen the Ghost Adventures episode invited Kane, R.a. and me to join them; however Kane was doing a movie, so R.a. and I joined them on a hunt at the Pico House. They had a pretty big group that was very interested in what had happened that night, so I began to walk them through the part of the building Nick and I had been in, I had my K2 meter out, which I usually have very good success with, but I might as well have taken the batteries, out, I was getting absolutely no responses, when an idea struck me.

Realizing that most of those killed in the riot would have been either Chinese or Mexican, I asked if anyone spoke Spanish. A girl said she could, so I asked her if she would wait ten seconds after what I said in English, and then repeat it in Spanish. Bingo! The lights were flashing four and five lights to the Spanish, which to me made this encounter even more credible, and actually taught me to try that on other hunts.

See? Every once in a while my brain works, and I get an inspired idea…Ok, you've waited long enough… I was telling the group about how Nick and I had been lured back and forth down the hallway, and about what sounded like very hard and loud running on steel stairs, but the only stairs at that end were cement…

One of the guys said "really? Follow me" and we headed to the area where we had heard the noise, and where the left hallway had been blocked off when we were there, it was now open, and the guy led us around the corner, pushed open a door that was at the front of the building and there was a set of steel stairs! Now remember, the security had cleared the building… See Nick Groff, we aren't crazy after all!

Kane, Nick Groff, R.a Mihailoff and Rick

Chapter 12
My Mom and I had an Awesome Bond

I was in high school when something unexplainable happened...

My mom and Gram shared one bedroom while I had the other. One night I had a horrible dream where I saw my mom sleeping in her bed when suddenly a gun, which looked like a 45 caliber was aimed at her from a person standing over her... I couldn't see any of the person, just the hand and the gun aiming at her... I jolted upright in bed, and then realized it was a dream... and then my mother screamed!

I went flying down the hall and ripped open her door, ready to defend her from whatever made her scream, obviously my adrenaline was pumping! When I went into the bedroom, she was sitting up in the bed, looking very scared, my Gram was awake, and she had heard the scream also.

There was no one else around, so I asked my mother what had happened... She said she had a bad dream, and there was a man with a gun standing over her with a 45 caliber pistol...

Part 2

Many years later I went back to Chicago to take care of my mom.

My mom was very ill, she had stage 4 lung cancer, and she had fought it for 15 years, I know that sounds impossible, but I went to her cancer Doctor with her many times, and he always called her his miracle patient.

As her time was waning, she had a hospice nurse named Tina that would sit with her, and she was a real angel on Earth, if you ever want to meet people who really care, the first one's you should see are the hospice nurses.

Her nurse was a small Philippino woman, and she couldn't have been sweeter to my mom, she was a real comfort to her and me.

I came in to see how my mom was doing, she was asleep, but looked to be in pain, and I don't know how, but I knew she wanted me to talk to her… and deep down I knew what she needed, and wanted, but it would be the hardest thing I have ever had to do… I needed to let her go..

I asked Tina if I could talk to my mom alone, and she went into the kitchen…

I went over and held my mom's hand, and told her I didn't like to see her suffering and that I knew she was hanging on for me… I told her not to worry about anything, that I would take of it… I told her if she got the chance to cross over I wanted her to go… I squeezed her hand for a bit, then went back into the kitchen, and Tina went back to sit with my mom…

I had been watching TV for a short while when I heard "Rick" come from the living room; I thought it was Tina, because my mom could barely talk above a whisper. When I got into the room, Tina was looking around with a confused look on her face. I asked her if she had called me, and she said no… but then she said I heard someone call you… Deep down I knew it was my mom telling me she had heard me. I went immediately to the phone and called my cousin Joyce, who was very close to my mom… She had told me she would come over on the weekend to see her, but I said if you want to see her, come now, and she hurried over…

When Joyce got there my mom woke up and they talked for a very short time, and then Joyce came and sat with me. I told her about hearing my name called out, and I knew that she was ready to let go... We talked for a while, Joyce went in and said goodbye to my mom, who was sleeping. I was glad she had come over, my mom loved Joyce...

That night as I headed up to get some sleep, I stopped on the stairs and said to Tina "call me". She knew what I meant, but she said she had just checked all her vital signs and she had a couple of weeks left... I smiled at her and softly said "please call me" and went up to bed...

A couple of hours had passed when I heard Tina shouting my name and I went running down the stairs, I could see my mom gasping for air... I ran up and grabbed her hand, she took a few more breaths, and then her suffering was over... I felt relieved that her pain was gone, and I have no doubt that her and Gram are together again, and that Heaven welcomed her...

Part 3

After the funeral we all had a chance to get together, and Joyce asked me if I felt the presence of my mom in the house, and I told her no, but I was positive she would find a way to say goodbye to me, and I was leaving early the next morning, I had been by her side for 4 months, and had a lot of stuff to catch up on in California...

I went to bed, my mom's room was one half of the attic, and it was on the third floor, so it is extremely dark up there.

I couldn't sleep, I was so restless knowing I had to get up very early to catch my flight... and I had a real sense of anticipation... As I was laying there I noticed a small glowing light about the size of a marble, with that greenish color of a tennis ball... It was very bright and my eyes were locked on to it, and it slowly grew in size until it got to be the size of a softball... I watched it hovering in the air for about 15 seconds when it suddenly shrunk and vanished!

I smiled to myself, and then said out loud, "Goodbye mom, I love you"

I told you we had an awesome bond!

Sometimes Kane Hodder gets a little extreme

Sometimes Kane Hodder gets a little extreme... who knew? While I was on the set of Hatchet there is a scene where Kane (as the character Victor Crowley) is to get hit in the face with a shovel by the lead actress. After she had done the swing by Kane's head, no contact involved, Kane asks Adam Green, the director, if he can get a shot of the shovel hitting his face, and Adam says OK.

Kane then asks me, because it will be a tight shot, and you wouldn't be able to see who was swinging the shovel to really hit him in the mug... I'm thinking, wait! Is it my birthday? I've always wanted to whack him with a shovel!

The shovel we were going to use was a prop made of hard plastic, they used it to cut off a head in an earlier scene, and had used it to dig a hole in the hard ground, so this was no wimpy rubber type prop, it was hard and well made..

They set up the shot, and Kane explains to me what he wants... he says hit me about a quarter speed on the side of his face, and he will drop down to a knee out of frame, and if he stands up and looks at me, to hit him harder....now I know some of you are thinking he has a mask on, how much can that hurt? The face was made of thin rubber so he could make facial movements for his character, so it would be like hitting your hand with a hammer while you were wearing gloves, in other words, it wouldn't help very much...

All kidding aside about whacking him, the last thing I want to do is hurt my friend by hitting him in the temple or the ear, so on the first swing I was extra careful, but still hit him pretty good, you could hear the smack all across the set… Kane takes the hit, drops to a knee for a second, then looks up at me and stands up, he gets back into the character stance, and I hit him much harder, and he drops to his knee out of frame.. I am starting to think he really is Victor Crowley, that whack should have rung his bell pretty good… I'm kind of afraid I might of hurt him by how hard I hit him, I could feel the impact up my arms, so I know I hit him hard and solid..

Kane shakes his head a few times then stands up again… I can tell he wants me to do it again…all he quietly says is kind of scary…" harder"… I hit him about as hard as you can, and the shovel breaks on his face! He goes to his knee, shakes his head, then stands up and laughs…

I believe if I ever write another book, the title of the book will be "**I BROKE A SHOVEL ON KANE HODDER'S FACE**"

Chapter 13
My First Scotland Trip

Scotland has beckoned to me from afar for all of my life, a calling that I was finally able to respond to, and I know it was a combination of my ancestors being from Scotland, the awesome ghost hunting locations, and just the idea of meeting new people and a new adventure that made me want to go so much. But there was one thing I was totally unprepared for... the Scottish people.

Rick, Bill Goldberg and Kane Hodder

I was working on a movie called Checkpoint in North Carolina with my buddy Kane, and we had to set up all kinds of action, gunfights, hand to hand combat and we worked our asses off, going from set to set to finish the movie.

After that then I had to go to Chicago to work on my mother's house so I could sell it.

I then went on to Nashville for the Home Show we run. Because of this, I had very little time to plan out my Scotland trip. Where to stay or where to go, so I was really in the dark, and never really had a chance to get excited about my trip being so busy with everything else.

Right after the Home Show, I flew to Chicago and spent a week clearing everything out of the house. I cleaned it top to bottom, it is three and a half stories, so it was pretty intense getting it done, I really worked my ass off!

Next I flew to Los Angeles, where I had a total of two days to grab everything and head off on the trip I had been waiting years for.

As I landed in Edinburgh and grabbed my bag, I headed up to a man who worked there and asked him where a cab would be. He asked me where I was going, and then told me the cab would cost fifty dollars, but if I went out front and grabbed the bus, it was only seven dollars! I jumped on that bus as quick as I could, then realized other than knowing the address of the Travelodge, I had no idea where I was going. I went up front and asked the driver, who told me he would call out to me when it was my turn to get off. After about a half an hour, he called me to the front of the bus, and I could see the hotel in front of me, about a block walk. Perfect! He said hold up mate, it's a bit tricky to find the entrance to the hotel, and you have to go down the side and in through the alley... It would have taken me quite a while to find it, but $43 dollars ahead of the game, thanks to very helpful people, I found the alley, and as I stood looking at the building I thought this hotel might not be what I was looking for as far as a place to stay, but I was totally wrong. . Without anywhere else to go, I headed in, where I met the desk clerk Alan. I told him I was there for my first real vacation, and he made sure I got a room with a view, and it was magnificent! It was a huge room, and check out the photo of my view!

I was also fortunate to meet Ana Lopes, who helped me get a room at another hotel when theirs was full, and Michal Maciag who guarded my luggage like a pit bull.   Once again, great people, extremely helpful.

Alan and I would chat a lot at that front desk, as he would tell me what to see and how to get there. I was right on the main street across from Edinburgh Castle, it was very busy with tourists, and you could walk most everywhere.

There were so many interesting things and so much history, you would walk up and down those hills all day and not realize you had probably done close to ten miles.. One thing I noticed walking up those hills, some fairly steep, is that the girls have definitely benefitted from walking all those hills... Hey, I'm single and on vacation, and I'm allowed to notice!

One place I was very anxious to see was Rosslyn Chapel, made famous in the DaVinci Code with Tom Hanks, and where many experts say the Knight's Templar hid the Holy Grail and the Ark of the Covenant.

Alan at the front desk of the Travelodge told me where to catch the bus, it was only about 150 yards from the hotel, and it was only three dollars to get to the chapel. It was a double decker bus, so of course I went up top to see the sights, and as I was riding along, once again I realized I didn't know where to get off. I asked the lady next to me if she knew what stop I should get off at, and she said she would tell me when to head downstairs. A bit later she said next stop. Dang, these people are so nice! I went down to the front of the bus and asked the driver how to get to the Chapel as he pulled to a stop... He chuckled, pointed straight ahead and said "go down that road, and you'll walk right in the front door..

Rosslyn Chapel

Yes, I realize Rosslyn Chapel and the city it resides in are spelled differently. Who knew? After I had exited the bus, I had a nice walk, only a couple hundred yards until I got to the Chapel...

It has a gift shop where you can grab a sandwich or something to drink, as well as a souvenir shop. I paid for my ticket, and headed onto the Chapel grounds.

I walked all around the Chapel, I was in no hurry at all, and I had wanted to come here for a long, long time, so I was enjoying all I could... I went into the Chapel, which isn't as big as I would have thought, but it was awesome!

The hand carved wood and stone work was amazing, and a lady walked in, had us sit in the pews, and told us the history of the place. I won't go into all of it, but one of the things that really caught my interest was a carving in the stone of what was obviously corn. Why is that interesting? I'm glad you asked... At the time the Chapel was built, no one had yet been to America, the only place corn grows.

Told you it was interesting! I went over everything, thinking I might actually be standing in the place where the Holy Grail and the Ark f the Covenant may have been. Something about the Chapel, its history, the whole surrounding area really felt like home to me, I know I have ancestors from Scotland, but I really liked this place.

If you go to the Chapel the grounds around it are full of cool things, the parts of a castle destroyed by the British, three old time cemeteries, and paths that will take you through the woods, you could spend a week investigating the place... And I did! I walked back up the road to catch my bus back to Edinburgh when I saw a small, very charming two story inn. I went in to look around..

The Chapel Cross Guesthouse

The inn was a very old period type, with a desk in the entry for the hotel, and to the right was a Tea Room. I wandered into it and was transported back to another time. There was a young girl named Beth there behind the counter, maybe 15, and dressed in a long, old time apron. I thought I had walked through a portal, what a great place!

I went to the counter and checked the menu, ordered a sandwich and an iced tea. The girl brought it over, and a lady came out of the kitchen. I was the only customer there, so we all talked while I ate.

Once again, the Scottish people are so nice! It dawned on me that this would be a great place to stay for a few days as I wanted to ghost hunt, and this place had the right look and feel. I asked the lady how much it would be to stay, and was nicely surprised, it was about half what I would have paid for the weekend in Edinburgh, so I told her I would be back the next day, jumped on the bus and went back to the city, spent the night wandering through it, checking out places to ghost hunt. I chose Edinburgh Castle to visit, man, that place is awesome!

It's enormous, and everything is pretty much the same from it was first built. OK history buffs, the English burned it down; all except for one room, but the Scots took it back and rebuilt it.

I was anxious to see it, because I am supposed to be related to King Malcolm, my last name comes from Malcolm, and I wasn't disappointed, I found four King Malcolm's on their Wall of Kings.(I think I should have gotten a discount on my admission)!

Back to the Chapel Cross Guesthouse

The next morning I grabbed my stuff, jumped on the bus, and made my way back to The Chapel Cross Guesthouse. When I got there, I met a lovely lady named Gail, who hooked me up with a nice room with a view of the Rosslyn Inn, and right outside the hotel is a courtyard that is next to their bar/restaurant, which is a meeting place for the locals (and tourists).. I had several dinners there; every one was excellent, as were the people who work there.

I met the owners of The Chapel Cross, Richard and Amy, really nice people who made sure I enjoyed my stay, especially the waffles I had every morning!

I had an adorable server named Abigail; I gave her one of our Hollywood Ghost Hunter shirts, and put her picture in our online magazine… This place was so comfortable for me, I ended up staying five days all together, and I am going back every time I go to Scotland.

The Guesthouse, as a matter of fact the entire area is a total gem of a place to kick back and just roam the countryside. I went to Rosslyn Chapel several times, went down to a field where William Wallace of Braveheart fame socked it out with the British, as well as a cave where he used to hide from the British. I love Roslin!

Chapter 14
Premier Paranormal Tours

I wrote on Facebook about wanting to go ghost hunting in Scotland, and if anybody there had any suggestions. I got a lot of great responses, including one from Gary Hughill.

He introduced me to another member of the group, his name is Brian Harley, who had some great suggestions on places to hunt around Edinburgh, so we agreed to meet when I got there.

Brian came to the Travelodge where I was staying, we grabbed a bite to eat and set up a game plan. Now, the first thing I noticed is that he was wearing a black trench coat and one of those black hats the bad guy always wear in the spy movies, and gave him a strong resemblance to Boris Badenov of Rocky and Bullwinkle fame.

OK, now that I have figured out what I'm going to call him, we set up a hunt at Haile's Castle for the following night.

Brian, AKA Boris came and got me, and he brought along Carol Ann Hosburgh, a really sweet girl who I would come to find out was totally fearless.

We headed out to the castle, which wasn't but about a half hour away, and as we went down this dark curvy road I asked them if we were going to get in trouble wandering around in the dark. He said Scotland is a lot more open when it comes to ghost hunting, so everything would be fine, last thing I want to do on my vacation is to get thrown into the hoosegow!

There were a few houses we went by, but when we got to the castle, it sat all alone in this big field, very isolated, very quiet with only the moon for illumination, it was classic! It was eerie moonlight, an abandoned run down castle, exploring time!

We walked about two hundred yards and as we got close, you could see parts of it had either been destroyed or caved in; it had been cleaned up, but a fantastic place for my first hunt in Scotland...

A quick tour of the castle showed it to be very large, with several different areas to explore. Choosing the bottom floor, we started our investigation, where we did voice recordings, EMF detectors, and carefully swept the entire room with my night vision camera, but it was very quiet, so we headed up to the room upstairs.

Where I was standing looking into the field

As we went up the stairs, I had a very strong feeling something was on the grounds with us, about a hundred yards away... Brian went down a ways to check, and when he got back, he said there was no one there.

Still, I could feel something out there, so I would look out the door from time to time. Nothing was happening on that floor so we went around to the back and down some stairs to an area where prisoners were held underground, there was a grate with a lock on it in the floor that led straight down for about eight feet.

Ghosts Believe in Me

Carol Ann lay down on her stomach and looked in. In all the time we were at the castle my K2 meter did not go up even a single light, and we were in the middle of nowhere with no electricity or outside influences that might make it go off, so were all got a major surprise when Carol Ann stuck her face against the grate and yelled "HELLO"... The K2 meter instantly lit up with all five lights flashing for about 10 seconds, as if she had scared something to flee from underground...

See, I told you she was fearless! After that, I had to give her a nickname, Carol Ann doesn't sound like a tough ghost hunting name, and so I started calling her the Castle Raider...

Leaving that area, we headed again to the top floor; once again I felt a presence about a hundred yards away in the tall grass, the same place as before.

We stopped and looked, and all of a sudden I see what looks like the light from one of those old fashioned lanterns that they used back in older times. I watched it; Boris and the Castle Raider finally saw it.

We were trying to figure out exactly where it was, the houses were that direction but much farther to the right across the road. While we were looking, the light started moving further into the tall grass, we watched it for maybe 10 seconds as it moved, and then it went out. Hard to imagine why anyone would be out there at roughly two in the morning, walk into field and then turn off their light, or even why I had felt them over there all night.. Very interesting...

We called it a night and they took me back to the Chapel Cross Guesthouse... We made plans to go to Greyfriars and the South Bridge Vaults.

I got picked up the next day by Brian, Carol Ann, and their friend Alex Power, and we hit Edinburgh.

Edinburgh at night is a great place to walk around; the Edinburgh Castle all lit up in the background, the entire city lights up all those historic buildings, hills and streets. You can let your imagination take you back in time; the history seems to wash over you in waves. I love the feeling you get here.

We first went to Greyfriars, a very famous cemetery surrounded by old time buildings and monuments. Brian told us there were thousands of people buried there, one of the most occupied cemeteries anywhere, but it is not like you think... most of the graves are behind a gate, so you can't really see them, but it is a really interesting place.

Brian and Alex were walking ahead of me and Carol Ann, it was fall, so there were lots of leaves on the ground, when we heard very distinct footsteps to our right, about twenty feet away. The sound went on for several seconds then stopped, but definitely something was up, as we both turned to look to see who was there. Nobody, nothing, the leaves weren't even moving. Nice start for the night!

Brian took us over to the City of Edinburgh Tours, where Josh took us first back to Greyfriars, a really remarkable place. It was cool to be on the tour, and Josh was an excellent guide.

We learned even more of the history of Greyfriars, and then it was on to the South Bridge Vaults. William led us on a tour of the underground vaults, and told us of a lady in white who appears at the end of the hallway on occasion, and dolls that move in another section.

Ghosts Believe in Me

One word of caution: if you are tall, pay attention as you go through doorways, the people were a lot shorter back when they built the vaults, I found that out by bashing my head in the dark... I should have listened to William, he warned us earlier!

The tour group filtered out, and a woman named Kelly came in and told us we had the place to ourselves, she was very nice, and told us some of the things that some of the people on tours had experienced, particularly the lady in white. (Why do they always wear white?)

I couldn't believe that we were getting this place to ourselves, and we started right in. The place where the lady in white was repeatedly seen was at the end of the hallway, and there were a few steps to go up, and ended about three feet high.

I asked them to turn out the lights and went up the stairs, crawled under the overhang and sat down cross legged on the floor, and then Carol Ann used my night vision camera to film it. I had a K2 meter and voice recorder, but was getting no results. After about fifteen minutes I looked out and Carol Ann was looking directly at me, still filming, when I noticed she was talking to someone.

I crawled from under the small room, and asked her who she was talking to. She said she had been talking to Brian, and she seemed shocked when I told her that while she was talking there was no one else in the tunnel, actually no one but me anywhere near her. She said she was positive someone was there, when right then Brian walked up from the other part of the vault. She asked if he had been standing right next to her and he said no, he was in the other room, as he and Alex had been trying to see if they could get the dolls to move, but no luck.

Carol Ann was absolutely positive someone had been standing next to her, but I told her I saw her the whole time she was filming, and she was always alone. Pretty cool! This place is getting some energy flowing!

We did some still photos next, they set up a laser grid in the tunnel, and I used my phone to snap some pictures, and I aimed my camera at the spot where they would see the lady in white. I began calling for the lady in white to come forward, … I snapped two pictures in a row; checking the first picture I saw nothing, but the second was an entirely different story, you can see them below…

The red dots are the laser grid. In the first picture the tunnel is clear, in the second picture there is something person sized in white at the end of the tunnel, right where people see the lady… Is it her? Or is it an anomaly of the camera? I'll let you make up your own mind.

#1 No object at the back

#2 A shape appears at the back

We started to wind down the hunt, when Brian suggested one more room. We searched it, and Carol Ann, Alex and I walked out and sat on a bench...

We could hear Brian talking in the other room. When he stepped out he saw me and looked startled. He said "how long have you been out here"? We told him we had all been there several minutes. Brian seemed perplexed, saying he had been talking to me in the other room, he thought I was standing next to him. Sound a little familiar? It is exactly the same thing that had happened to Carol Ann.

Now these are no newbies when it comes to ghost hunting, so I think it has a good deal of credibility, they are not the types to make things up or mistake someone standing next to them. I wonder if other people that have gone there have had the same experience.

The following day Boris and Carol Ann stopped by the Guesthouse to chat, and I told them of all the things I'd seen around Rosslyn Chapel, but the one thing I missed but really wanted to see was the cave where William Wallace of Braveheart fame would hide while the British were hunting for him. I'd tried to find it, no luck, and one of the guides at the Chapel said there was a landslide, a lady broke her leg and you couldn't get there right now. Boris immediately said "come on, I'll show it to you".

We jumped in his car and drove to a farm type place and got out. I said is it OK to be on this property? He said you needed permission, and he had it, so the three of us went about a quarter of a mile when we came to a steep downslope which turned into about a fifty foot drop.

We proceeded slowly and very carefully. As we reached a granite slab we stopped and looked at the view, which was fantastic. I realized I was on the other side of the creek from Rosslyn Chapel and never would have been able to find this place on my own. I looked to Boris and said "I don't see a cave", he chuckled and said "you're standing on it".

Boris led me and the Castle Raider down and around the granite to a steep down slope again, only this one went right to the edge of the drop off, and the fall would definitely put a severe hurting on you, at least. There was a path about two feet wide that went from the rock face on one side, and the drop on the other, so we moved very carefully for about thirty feet and there it was.. We went in, it was bigger than I thought it would be, and I can see why no one ever found him, it was almost impossible to find, very easily defended, all he had to do was poke anyone who tried to come with his sword and they would fall over the drop off. We checked it out for a while then made our way back to the Guesthouse.

Sadly, it was time for me to return to Hollywood, but I am sure we will be friends for a very long time!

Brian Harley and Carol Ann Hosburgh    Hailes Castle

Chapter 15
The Nicest Ladies in All of Scotland

Carolyn, Rick and Isobel

    I had been to Scotland several years in a row, and had made friends with people at the Travelodge in Edinburgh, Alan Robertson in particular, and at The Chapel Cross Guest House in Roslyn, where I got to know Richard and Amy, the owners of the Inn.

    I had made only made reservations for the first three days, as I planned to go several different places, and there are a lot of places to stay. That was my first mistake.

    I went to the Chapel Cross to see about staying the weekend and Amy said they were all booked, so I asked her if there were any other places nearby. She had a strange look on her face and proceeded to tell me that there was not a hotel room to be had between Edinburgh and Glasgow, due to the European Rugby Championship.

Aaron Glen Guesthouse

She suggested I call Carolyn Davidson at the Aaron Glen Guest House close by. I hopped on the bus back to Edinburgh, checked with Alan at the Travelodge who confirmed they had no rooms, and neither did anyone else.

I knew there wasn't much hope but I called Carolyn at the Aaron Glen. A very nice lady answered, it was Carolyn and I asked her about a room. She said she was very sorry, but they were full up. I guess the disappointment in my voice came through and she asked what was wrong. I told her I had saved for a year for my vacation which was supposed to last three weeks, and it looked like I was going to have to fly home after only three days. She asked me for my cell number and told me she would call me back. I had started checking for available flights home when she called. She said she didn't know if I would be interested but her mum was going to England for two weeks and she said I could use her house while she was gone.

I politely asked her how much that would cost and she said "don't you dare try to offer her money or she'll get mad"

I was absolutely speechless, and if you know me that is almost impossible to do.

My first thought was: who would do that? Let a person they've never met stay for free in their house while they are gone? It was almost impossible to process how incredibly kind and generous that was. I accepted their gracious offer, and when I left there after my stay there were two bottles of champagne on the counter, and I had cleaned up after myself better than I had ever cleaned in my life.

I became friends with Carolyn, her husband Les and her wonderful mum Isobel, and made a point to stay at the Aaron Glen for three days last year, and I'm going there again this year! What wonderful people!

I took Isobel and Carolyn out to dinner while I was there; I mean how can you ever repay a kindness like that? They are Angels on Earth, without question.

There was a strange occurrence while I stayed at the house. I had come back late to the house after ghost hunting a castle with some friends, and as I walked into the kitchen I heard splashing sounds, there was water on the floor that I had just walked in.. I turned on the lights and saw the water, so I searched everywhere in the kitchen for where the water could have come from.

The sink was too far away, the washer hadn't been on, and I couldn't find the source of the water, and then I looked at the stove. On the burner there was a half-moon of water, the best way to describe was that it looked like a pot had boiled over. I did no cooking while I was there, and hadn't put anything at all on the stove. The water could not have come from the sink as it was too far away. I noticed a carpenters pencil on the edge of the stove, and I know for a fact it hadn't been there earlier, as I had cleaned the entire stove top, and wiped down the counters.

The next day I called Carolyn and asked if she or any of her workers had been in the house, she said no, but the carpenters pencil intrigued her, as her father had been into woodworking.

It remains a mystery to me, but I will never forget my two Scottish ladies! (Or Les who makes the breakfasts at the Inn and every one looks like it was made in a 5 star restaurant)! God Bless all three of them!

Chapter 16
Even I can't believe it!

Several years ago my friend Adam Green called me and gave me the part of Silent John, one of the hunters that go into the swamp to kill the homicidal maniac Victor Crowley in the second installment of the Hatchet movies, aptly named Hatchet 2.

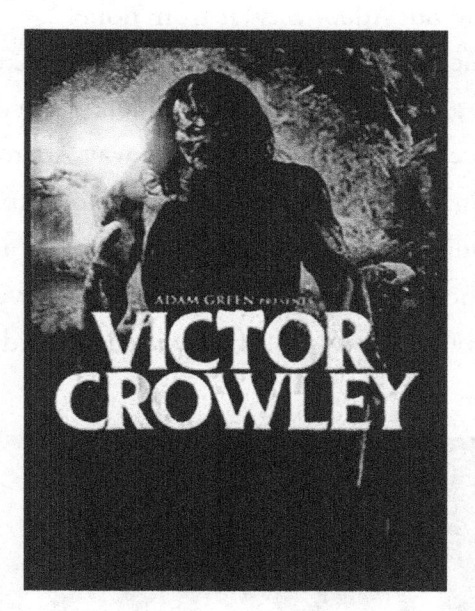

The movie was a hell of a lot of fun to work on, when Adam Green directs a film, he puts everything he has into it, and one of the coolest things you could ever see is how excited he gets when he gets a great scene. For those of you who don't know about the Hatchet movies, and how you could not, they were some of the bloodiest, goriest amazingly horrifying deaths in horror history. When Kane Hodder plays Victor Crowley you know it's going to be action packed, with very inventive methods of kills, and very, very messy... To say the least!

My character, Silent John never says a single word in the movie, I think it was because Kane and Adam just wanted to shut me up for a while, but I did get to mouth three little words into the camera when Victor Crowley comes out of the swamp bushes with a chainsaw with an eight foot blade going full speed!

What werethe three words? Come on, really? What else could you possibly say than WTF? I loved that the audience at the premier got a big kick out of it, but Adam was far from done!

Kane puts the chainsaw between my legs, and Colton's legs as well, lifting us off the ground and sawing us in half... from the crotch through the top of the head! To do this scene the way Adam wanted it, it had to be extraordinarily bloody, so to get the blood really flying Robert Pendergraft, the Special Effects supervisor placed a blood cannon in front of me, when one of the assistants came over and started filling it, stopping about halfway full, then asked me did I think that was enough blood…

I asked him "you know Adam, right?", so he filled it up to the top... when we were shooting the shot Colton and I were suspended in midair, Kane ramming the chainsaw into our crotches like a madman, and the blood cannon goes off and blood is absolutely flying everywhere, we were so covered in blood, and this is not even a slight exaggeration, that when we were done with the scene and I went to take a shower, because SFX blood and leather car seats area bad combination, that when I had all my clothes off there was not one single inch of my body that wasn't covered in blood including the bottom of my feet!

Now, movie blood doesn't come off very easy so you need to use Barbasol shaving cream to really scrub it off, I got enough off to not get any on my car seats, but it took several cans to get it all off... Oh the glamorous life of movie making...

The next question is was Adam Green done with the surprises for me? Not by a long shot...

A Red Carpet, photographers and interviewers all over the place, the world famous Egyptian Theater was absolutely rocking with fans, celebrities and people having a great time.

The movie started, I was sitting in the balcony along with some of the Hatchet peeps... I am enjoying the heck out of the movie, anxiously waiting to see how the chainsaw death scene looked when the chainsaw starts up and I mouth my three little words, and was very happy with the crowd reaction...

And now comes Adam's surprise, as we are being chain sawed there is a close up of my crotch, blood flying when suddenly two balls start to hang down! Wait! Those are my balls!

Apparently Adam added that in post-production, and I never knew! The crowd started howling, and they dropped even farther, finally hitting the ground and the howl was even louder! OK Adam, I got to admit it was pretty cool, people in the theater started looking over at me and smiling like crazy!

Well done Mr. Green! You might think that is the reason for the title of this story, but it's not… As part of the promotion for the film the cast all went to Dark Delicacies, a cult favorite bookstore for movie poster signings and we all sat at a series of tables all lined up so people could start at one end and go on down the line to the next person to get their poster signed…

This is where the title of this story comes into play…

Two guys had just come up to my spot and asked if I would sign their poster and I replied" I would be happy to"… no sooner had the words come out of my mouth when the two looked very startled… I asked them what was wrong and one of them said the most incredible thing I've ever heard, they both look at me and one of them says "you can't talk!"

I laughed, thinking they were kidding, when I realized they were serious… I smiled and said "I can talk, I probably talk too much"… well, these guys were having none of it, one of them insisted a Hatchet 2 fan site had said I was mute…I told them that was not correct… the guy still argued, "you can't talk"! I just smiled and said "you realize I'm talking to you right now, right"?

Chapter 17
Frozen by a Hellish Growl… In Broad Daylight

Many ghost hunters believe that if you hear a growl near you while you're ghost hunting that it is the sign of something demonic. I'm not sure that's exactly true but I have been growled at on five different occasions, where someone else also heard the growl. The first place I was growled at was Waverley sanatorium in Kentucky; I followed a shadow into an empty room, when a very deep growl came up behind me. The two other hunters that were with me were standing in the doorway having just arrived there, and I asked them if they had heard the growl. The look on their face said it all, as they nodded their heads up-and-down so fast I thought they were going to black out.

The path to Rosslyn Chapel at night

I have also been growled at in Linda Vista Hospital, the William Heath Davis House in San Diego, and most recently right outside Rosslyn Chapel in Scotland

Where I heard the growl

The chapel is located in a much wooded area; it also has a gift shop in a small cafe attached where you actually go in to the chapel, and outside there is a 200 yard road that goes into the little village. The road is straight and you can see from the chapel all away into town, so it's very easy to see if there's anybody up in front of you. After investigating around the chapel one day and having lunch in the cafe I made my way back towards the little village, and as I was walking there were two older ladies in front of me, that I passed by and said hello.

I was looking at a very old building on the left, where most of the famous people of Scotland and England had actually visited ,when I heard directly in front of me about 15 feet away the most ungodly growl that sounded like a combination of a grizzly bear and an attack dog. I froze, totally still, afraid that if this dog was close by it was going to attack me, and slowly turned my head back to look down this street and there was absolutely nothing there no people, no dogs. I looked down the side streets and there were no people or animals, and as I stood there the two ladies walked up to me, looked at me and said we heard it too.

Later I walked eight miles through the Roslyn Forest back to the house I was staying in, and I waited for a light to change.

I had made it into the city of Eskbank by this time, and started to be concerned about the growl I had heard, most ghost hunters consider them demonic, and I have absolutely no other way to describe it. As I stood there I said to myself "I think I could use a little backup with this growling thing" As I looked down, this is what I saw…

My shadow

This Still Makes Me Wonder

Several years ago I had a Toyota Forerunner which I had decided to give to the Salvation Army. It had beautiful chrome Crager mag wheels that were worth a fair piece of change, along with Michelin tires, and the truck was in really good shape, but it had some engine problems a good mechanic could fix. I was just ready for a bigger SUV to haul stunt equipment in.

The mag wheels had locks on them, and I had already scheduled the Salvation Army pick up time, which was only a couple of hours away. As I was emptying out my stuff, I knew that whoever got the car would need the special lug nut that would take off the locks, or they wouldn't be able to take off the tires. I t would be really bad if you got a flat on the highway and couldn't change a tire.

The lug nut adapter was pretty much the same size as a lug nut, a little bigger, and round, similar to a socket. I had put it into the tool kit that stayed in the back storage well. I opened the well and took out the tool kit, which was made of plastic that you could roll out flat to select what tool you wanted to use. It was only about a foot long and about eight inches high, not big at all.

I rolled the kit out flat, but I could see that the adapter wasn't in it… I took out the tools, they slide into small pockets, and laid the tool kit completely flat, and completely empty. I doubled checked by patting the kit to make sure it was totally empty, and it was. I picked it up and shook it, and there was no weight to it at all. It was absolutely empty.

Sadly, I put the tools back in and rolled it up and put it back in the well. I felt really bad that I would be giving the truck to charity, and they would have to have the locks removed. I stood there quietly for a few moments, and then I said out loud, " I really want the Salvation Army to make some money, please help me find the adapter."

I knew deep down I had put it in the tool kit, and opened the well, removed the toolkit and opened it. Directly in the center sat the adapter…

Chapter 18
Spirit on a bicycle in Brentwood Tennessee

My dad was in the hospital when my stepmother Vandy and I got a call at about four in the morning saying that my dad was getting combative and demanded a phone, which he promptly used to call a limousine to pick him up (even sick my old man had style!). The nurses begged us to hurry down to the hospital to calm him down as he was dead set on leaving and no one was going to stop him. Vandy and I jumped into my truck and headed down there. My dad and Vandy lived in Brentwood, a pretty upper scale area where a lot of the country singers lived, and it was a rural area, very quiet, and as we turned down this long two lane road my attention was caught by something in the road a couple of hundred yards ahead.. It appeared to be someone on a bicycle, but there were no houses or roads for the bike to have come from... I stared at the image as we got closer and suddenly it looked like it reared up on the back tire, spun several times in a circle like an ice skater spinning and vanished! I looked at Vandy and said "did you see that?" She just looked at me and said "the guy on the spinning bike"? We looked along the side of the road to make sure the guy didn't have an accident... no guy, nowhere to be found! Right then the hospital called and said they had sedated my dad and he had fallen asleep. Vandy and I always wondered if that was my dad trying to get home and when he saw us went back to the hospital, none of this on an actual bike, but in his mind trying to get home. I don't know what it was, I can't explain it... but we both saw it clear as could be...

Saved by a French Whore

Many years ago, roughly twenty I would guess, I was driving my Toyota Forerunner from Denver to Nashville. My dad had passed away a few years before so I was thinking about him as I drove.

I was on a major highway, just cruising along and singing with the music, something I guarantee you don't want to hear, I sound like someone torturing a cat, and no, I'm not kidding!

I was making good time, and it was a beautiful sunny day and I was zooming along in the speed lane going about 70 MPH. I looked ahead of me and there was one of those big double tanker trucks, the kind that deliver gasoline. The truck was in the lane next to me on the right and as I got closer I noticed these very large cement dividers, the kind they use on highways to block traffic from going into another lane. As I closed up close to the truck from out of nowhere my brakes locked up! I wasn't touching them, but the brakes locking up caused me to fish tail and as I struggled to control the truck I was almost up to the tanker, all I could see was the tanker a little in front and on my right, and those huge cement barriers on the left. All of a sudden the tanker veers hard left, exactly where I would have been if the brakes hadn't locked up, and smashed up against the barriers. The tanker was in front of me, but I had slowed because of the brakes and pulled the wheel hard to the right, hoping nobody was coming up behind me in that lane, and thankfully it was clear. I went past the rear end of the tanker and the brakes unlocked, and I was able to regain control of my truck, my hands were shaking so badly from adrenaline I could barely hold the wheel. I knew that if the brakes hadn't locked I would absolutely have been killed. I said quietly "thank you" and the car filled up with the scent of Aramis cologne, which my dad wore in copious amounts, you could actually smell him coming from his bedroom down the hallway if you were in the living room. I would always tease him, hollering down the hallway "here comes the French whore"!

Good looking rascal, my dad!

The Bedroom Battle

I thought long and hard about telling this story, not sure how it would be received, but then I thought that I am writing a book about strange things that have happened to me, and this one certainly qualifies!

I was lying in bed, and I wasn't quite asleep. I felt something brush my ankle, but I thought it was just the comforter settling, so I didn't even move.

Suddenly I felt a hand wrap around my ankle and pull me towards the end of the bed. It wasn't a strong or dramatic pull, but then it pulled harder, and I jerked up in the bed just as the hand let go…

As long as I live I'll never forget what I saw... I saw the back of my father locked in a vicious struggle with something I couldn't see! The absolute best way to describe it is it looked two NFL linemen shoving each other. My dad was pushed backwards towards me as I jumped out of bed to help him, fully realizing I was looking at his spirit.

My father gave one last shove, driving back whatever had been after me, and then they vanished...

Could I have been dreaming? I really don't think so; because I saw at least 5-10 seconds of a titanic fight, all while I was jumping out of bed, fully awake...

On The Set with the Hollywood Ghost Hunters

As most of you know, and if you didn't you will now because you are reading this, is that the members of the group are all in some way connected to horror movies, we have actors, stuntmen, directors, special effects make up experts, writers, and producers. This story is about Kane Hodder, Ra Mihailoff and me on the set of the movie Hatchet 2.

The three of us were sitting in Ra's dressing room at Occidental studios; his dressing room was an actual room on the first floor... Ra began telling us this joke, using a fine Irish brogue to embellish the story... As he neared the end of the joke, he was hollering "God will get you", when directly behind him, out the window was the loudest crack of lightning, the flash filled the room... We all looked at each other, the look on R.a.'s face was priceless, the timing of the lightning could not have been better, and we laughed our asses off for about ten minutes... What is the moral of this story? Apparently R.a. has the best sound and lighting effects guy ever...

Strange Things at the William Heath Davis House

Several years ago I had invited Rick from the Hollywood Ghost Hunters to join my group, the San Diego Ghost Hunters on an investigation of the William Heath Davis House, a popular attraction in the Gaslamp District.

Rick came to the door, it was our first time meeting, and as I looked down the hallway a shadow crossed it into a room at the end of the hallway, I told Rick what I had seen, and off he went! I caught up to him just after he had gone in the room, and heard a very loud angry growl! Rick just said "don't worry, I get that a lot"... I guess he does, because as I was talking to him on the phone about a year later I heard another growl through the phone, and yelled. Rick asked what happened and I told him about the growl... He just laughed and said "I told you it happens a lot"...On another occasion at the William Heath Davis House, we were all sitting on the living room floor doing a spirit box session when the box spit out the words "outside", "men", "beware" "wasted and "police"

I looked out the window of the front door and three men were trying to get in the gate to take the Christmas lights. I told them it was private property and they couldn't come in. They were obviously drunk and wouldn't take no for an answer. They started getting more loud and insistent, I stood my ground.

Rick came out the house and told them to leave and they said" who's going to stop us"? Rick smiled and said "me, now beat it before we call the cops". They cursed at us and left, but how strange was it that the spirit box warned us they were out there?

Maritza Skandunas, San Diego Ghost Hunters

More Wierdness at the House

I was pushed on a staircase in San Diego, and only the fact that I was starting to sit down kept me from going down the stairs headfirst... of course I've been doing movie stunts for over 30 years, so I would have been OK..

Brandi Leigh at the William Heath Davis House

Rick and I were investigating the William Heath Davis house in downtown San Diego along with the ladies from San Diego Ghost Hunters. After a couple of hours Rick and I were going over some findings, I was sitting down at the top of the staircase, he was standing just a couple steps down from me. As we were talking I see Rick start to go backwards down the stairs. It wasn't an oops I lost my balance scenario; you could see his body being shoved down. There's a large difference between being clumsy and the way your body reacts to being shoved by another person, in this case, an entity. After regaining his balance we went and got the ladies to explain what had just happened. About an hour or so later Rick and I were leaving for both of our long treks home, still amazed about the night's findings, the ladies stayed for a while longer. Maritza decided to get the Spirit Box out and see if they could get an answer to who shoved Rick. "Who pushed Rick?" The response was a loud and clear "spirits." They followed up with "spirits? How many spirits pushed Rick?" The answer? "Five"! When asked why so many, the box said "he's big" ☺. Turns out like most of the spirits in the house, these were not trying to hurt him; they just wanted to see what would happen. Crazy crazy! I'll stick with the spirit of the doctor who says I'm pretty and asks me to stay ☺

Ghosts Believe in Me

Brandi Leigh and Rick

Chapter 19
The Sword

When my dad passed away my evil stepmother gave me his collection of Franklin Mint swords (ok, she really isn't even a little bit evil), and it is a good reminder of my dad and I like them a lot... but... I was sitting in my office working on the computer when I heard a loud crash in my living room, and ran out to it expecting to see a burglar. I didn't expect what I found... Lying the across the room, roughly nine feet away from the wall was one of the swords. Now this is a very large sword with a heavy wooden display board behind it, and weighs probably around twenty to twenty five pounds, which is pretty heavy to attach to the wall, so I took extra care when I put it up, using two very strong hangers. After I had hung it, I grabbed on top of the wood and leaned my weight into it, and it didn't budge, so it was very secure on the wall, absolutely no way it could fall off the wall, as it had hooks on the hanger so that you had to lift it several inches to take it down. The only way it could have fallen was if the wall anchors had pulled out of the wall, so I checked them and they hadn't budged and were still in there very strong.

What in the world was going on here? Many people have seen shadows, and in one case a full body apparition in my apartment, so I know something is here, but why throw the sword?

That wasn't the only thing that had me wondering. From the distance and the position it was on the floor there is no way it could have gone that far. If you look at the picture, the sword I'm referring to is the large one in the middle with the big candle holder directly beneath it, only about four inches away. Had that sword fallen there is no way that candle holder wouldn't have been knocked over, and it hadn't been moved an inch. But the story gets even more mysterious!

Several weeks after the sword ended up across the room, I was sitting next to the little desk you can see in the picture when a movement caught my eye. I turned and looked and couldn't believe what I was seeing. A thick red stream was rolling down the wall, it stopped, leaving a thick line roughly a foot long. I reached out and touched it, it was slightly sticky and thick, and it felt and looked exactly like blood. Now most people would immediately wash it off, but I left it for people to see. If you look directly under the sword you can see it.

A few years later a friend of mine who does special effects make up for movies, meaning he makes the masks and applies all the creepy make up you see in movies, as well as all the blood.

He looked at it for me, asked if he could take the sword down and look at the back of it, of course I said yes. He carefully looked it over and finally said he didn't see anything that could have caused it...

The Little Girl in the Window

As you may have read by now I actually fell and really messed up my knee in Roslyn forest in Scotland. It is feeling a whole lot better because I try to walk at least 2 to 3 miles every day, and I found that it's exactly 2 1/2 miles from my house to the market and back where I get my sandwich every day.

I usually take the same route all the time and I've been going by this one house that looks totally out of place on Laurel Canyon. The house is gray, the paint is peeling badly and the hedges and plants are totally overgrown and have not been trimmed or anything for months.

The house has 2 stories, and on the 2nd story there are 2 windows, which I would guess are probably the windows of bedrooms. I always look at that house as I go by, there's just something about it that draws me to it, and one day as I was passing I was drawn to look up and I saw a young girl probably 10 or 11, wearing what look like in a white Easter dress. I noticed she was looking at me so I waved, but it was very strange she didn't move at all. She continued looking at me so I waved again, this time she gave me a very little wave.

I didn't want to seem like a creepy old man so I made my way back home. Several weeks later I was walking to the market and was surprised to see a young couple and a young boy had moved into the house and they were out in front working on the hedges and really trying to spruce up the place. They saw me looking at the house and made a comment that it is looking better isn't it? It still had the peeling paint but with the plants being cut down and some maintenance being done it was looking a lot better. A young boy was playing in the yard. I told them that I had seen their daughter about 2 weeks ago and waved at her up in the window. They looked at me with a very strange look and said we don't have a daughter. I asked if they knew the people who had lived there before and they told me that it had been vacant for quite a while and they were positive that nobody had been in the building because there were padlocks on the doors and you couldn't open the windows. That was several years ago and I've noticed that the hedges are all out of control again and the house looks totally abandoned, so I think I'm just going to look up there every time I go by and see if I can see my little friend.

I hope to see her again someday, and know that she is OK…

Chapter 20
The Queen Mary

I have been to the world famous Queen Mary ship many times, and have had access to the most haunted of places on the ship. I, along with R.a. Mihailoff, that cuddly little 6'5", 335 pound Leatherface actor, joined Zak Bagans, Aaron Goodwin, and several of the Ghost Adventures crew for dinner, which was a great time, and then we went off to an auction they were having for a charity.

I bumped into Chris Fleming, a friend of mine who has been on several TV shows, Ghost Hunters, Paranormal Children to name just a couple. I got a Spirit Box from him; he also has an online ghost hunting store, Ghost Outlet, where I get some of our equipment. The guys were hosting a ghost hunt and they had a very good crowd, and R.a. and I didn't want to get in the way, so we said our goodbyes.

It wasn't the last time R.a. and I were there, as we were guests on the live Halloween broadcast of Coast to Coast AM with George Noory... It was a great interview, it always is with George, he doesn't just ask the basic questions that we have all heard before, so I always enjoy being on his show.

![George Noory, Rick McCallum, R.A. Mihailoff — Coast to Coast AM]

The last time I was there wasn't long ago, I went with my evil stepmother Vandy and her boyfriend. As we walked around many people came up to us to talk ghost hunting, I was wearing my Hollywood Ghost Hunter t-shirt, so it wouldn't be hard to spot me, most of them had seen us on Ghost Adventures and wanted to know if I was going to hunt the ship that night. Repeatedly I was asked if they could come... I told them I would be out on the deck late at night, and if they saw me they were welcome to come along. I guess they really wanted to ghost hunt, because while I was out there, during the two hours I was out there, 14 people, not all at once, but in small groups went with me. We didn't have many experiences, but we all had a great time, I always enjoy meeting new people, so I considered the night well spent.

Ghosts Believe in Me

All these nights were fun, but the absolute best happened WHEN I WASN'T GHOST HUNTING!

Years ago my mom came to visit me, and she wanted to stay on the Queen Mary one night. Most people don't know that it is a hotel, so we drove down to Long Beach. When we boarded the ship there were a bunch of girls in prom dresses in the lobby just looking in the shops and checking out the restaurant at the bow. We grabbed our bags and walked forever to our room, the Queen Mary is huge!

After we got settled my mom asked me to get her a donut from the bakery, which, sadly is no longer there. I opened the door and was leaning on the door jamb asking what kind of donut she wanted, and what she wanted to drink. While I was leaning there I heard, very clearly, what sounded like ten to twelve young people, giggling, laughing and chatting as they came down the hallway. I turned to look down the hallway, it is very long, and I would guess from our room I could see about 100 yards down the hall. I could still hear the group coming, I figured they were about twenty yards away, I figured it was probably the kids from the prom. Surprise! The hall was absolutely empty for as far as I could see.

Being the curious ghost hunting type that I am, I hurried down the hallway, going in each alcove to see if they had gone into one of the rooms, listening, and then quickly moving on. I checked all the way down the hallway, not a sound from any room, and I had gone much farther than they could have travelled. I asked myself two questions; 1: Could they have gone anywhere else, and could I have heard them from the other floors? The answer was no... 2: Does anybody really believe a bunch of kids partying could go silent that quickly, and not a sound heard from them the rest of the evening?

Rick McCallum

Mom and me… We kind of look related!

Chapter 21
Excerpt from Kane Hodder Interview in Hollywood Ghost Hunters magazine

I will say one of the things that you and I have done I am most proud of is when we drove with the girl standing between the two cars, like they did in Footloose.

Kane: For sure, stunt wise...

Rick: I have to explain what happened a little. We were recreating the shot from Footloose where Lori Singer stands on top on the cars as they go down the street, one foot on each car. We had a stunt girl named Hannah Scott, who has was absolutely awesome, she was as cool as a cucumber up there, and we actually were going 42 miles an hour around curves.. She was harnessed, but it is still dangerous and had to be scary as hell but she performed spectacularly...

Rick driving the black car, Kane driving the green car

After we had done that we had to do a scene where Kane and I drag race in the forest, where one would be winning, then the other would pass and cut them off... We were following the camera truck which is also moving, and has a camera and operator on a boom arm on the back.

We take off, following the truck, and race beside each other, with us taking turns cutting the other off and taking the lead. I look up and see we are coming up fast on the camera truck, Kane is on my left and all of a sudden he heads directly at my driver's side wheelwell, just flying... I react by yanking the steering wheel to the right and he barely misses me and with very little room to spare he heads right toward the camera, which is low enough for him to hit. He slams on the brakes and goes sliding right towards the camera, the cameraman booms it up quickly and Kane slides right under it to a stop... It was awesome!

Rick: When you went by me I never thought you were going to make it...

Kane: The camera was too low for me to fit under there so I had to assume that the boom operator would counter my move and he did. That's probably the best driving stuff we've ever done. Old 37 was the movie...

Rick: The thing that got me is I had two actresses in the car, I was driving the convertible, and on the last one I'm looking at the camera truck ahead of us and I'm thinking, boy is this going to be close, and I was expecting you to cut in front of me and all of a sudden you went right at my wheelwell and I jerked the car to the right and you went sliding right under the camera, but I remember the most is the two actresses in my car were just screaming bloody murder. I hope they got that on tape because they couldn't get better screams. I was watching from behind and when you slid under that and I just went holy shit!

Kane: The best thing about it was none of us expected to do it.

Rick: The director made up the shot on the fly because we had a little more time left with the camera truck, he told us what he wanted and off we went...

Kane: It wasn't planned in any way but I had the faith in you to react to it, and the faith in the cameraman to react to it...

Rick: The best part is when we went back to the video village, for those not in the film business, video village is where the monitors are, usually the director watches from there, and as we drove up the whole crew was clapping and cheering, and that's when you know it looked pretty good... I remember the director saying Kane I thought you were going to tear the front of Rick's car off, and you said Rick won't let me hit him, and I wouldn't let him hit me. I remember walking away and whispering to you and said I wish you would have told me about that, and we both started laughing.

Sometimes I just can't explain it!

As you know, my only real superpower is that people are real nice to me... This is another time...

I was doing a movie in the Hamptons with Kane, which sounds really cool, you getting to hang around on the beaches with the super-rich beautiful people. Unfortunately we were shooting in late November and early December, and it is very cold in New York at that time of year, and a great deal of the shooting was outside. And the town was almost empty.

We were going to shoot a scene where a girl stands on the doors of two cars, like the famous scene in Footloose, as they go over forty miles an hour around curves, which involved some serious driving by Kane and me. We had to make sure the stunt girl was harnessed so she couldn't fall off, so I was running the cord to harness her with, and was under the car connecting several points so it would be strong and safe. Kane came over with the Director, Christian Winter, who was also concerned with the stunt girl's safety.

We had her get up on one of the cars and lean out into space, she had one leg out like she was on both cars and she was really solid.

As I crawled out from under the car, Kane started kidding me about my coat, a very old, forty years old roughly, and it had sewing on the outside where I had patched it over the years.

Christian asked why I didn't have a better coat, and I told him I could only wear a coat with a nylon shell, and couldn't find a warm one with long enough arms... I have arms like an orangutan, so it makes finding clothes very difficult.

Kane the said "did you really have to wear that ugly old piece of crap?" Now I took no offense, because Kane and I pick on each other a lot, always in fun, so I said seeing as I was crawling around under the car I didn't want to get my tuxedo dirty, so I thought my beat up old coat might be better for the job at hand. They cracked up, and we went off to lunch.

A few days later the wardrobe girl called me in and said I had a package. I told her I didn't order anything, and she smiled and said it had my name on it. I picked it up, and sure enough it did. Very curious I carefully opened it, and inside was a brand new black down jacket with nylon outer and very long arms. I tried it on, and it fit perfectly!

I asked the wardrobe girl where it had come from, and said Christian, the Director had seen it online when he was looking for a coat for himself, and when he saw it he bought it as a gift for me.

I went to Christian and thanked him for the very kind gesture, and offered to pay for it, as I was happy I would have a warm coat from this century that actually looks great and really fit nice.(if you have seen the pictures or videos of me in Scotland, I have that jacket on whenever it is cold!)

Christian wouldn't let me pay for it; he said he was happy to do it...

(Truth be told, if I didn't have the money for a warm coat Kane would've got me one)

Once again my only superpower led me to another Angel on Earth! Thank you Christian Winters!

On another film Kane not only got me on Charlie's Farm in Australia, he managed to pull off something great for me..

When the producers had originally scheduled the movie, they changed the shooting dates, and apparently they had forgotten about changing my plane ticket home, and I was to be there another week, a week after shooting was finished. I talked to the producer who told me I could stay at the compound, absolutely alone, with no TV, radio or anyone to hang out with… it didn't sound like a lot of fun.

Kane was staying in this fabulous condo right on the beach in Coolum, a totally fantastic spot. Kane went to the owner and talked him into letting me stay for the week!

Kane is a good dude, except for that little part about killing more people on screen than anybody in movie history!

I heartily suggest you check out To Hell and Back: The Kane Hodder story.. I have known Kane since 1982, and I was astounded at some of the stuff he went through, and I'm proud to say he is my friend, and it is easily one of the best and most emotional documentaries I've ever seen.

Rick McCallum

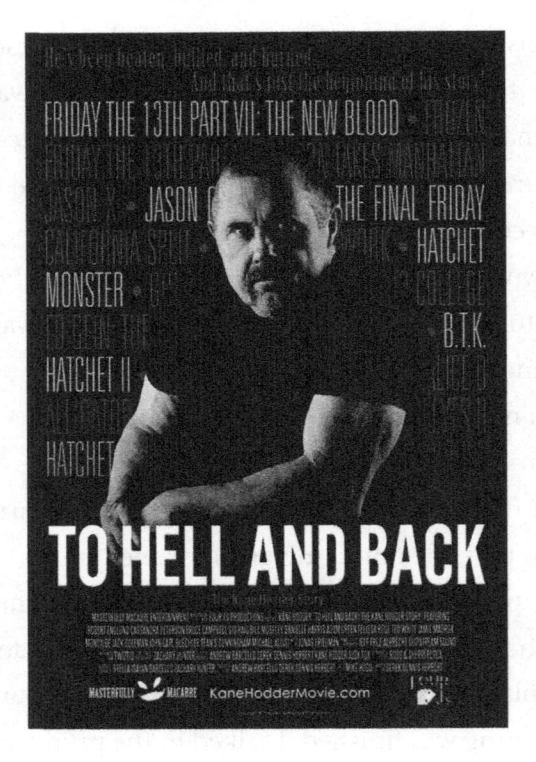

Chapter 22
Sometimes I Just Can't Help Myself!

I was in Mansfield Ohio, at Mansfield Reformatory working with Kane and R.a. on a movie named Fallen Angels. I played several characters, got to kill a lot of people; I even got to smash down a door, knocking a man to the ground, then hold him down and use a knife to pop his teeth out in one of the most brutal scenes I've ever seen! Loved it!

The movie starred Kane, R.a., Bill Moseley, Michael Dorn, Michael Berryman, Christopher Knight (Peter Brady from the Brady Bunch), Martin Kove and many others...

One of my scenes involved me as one of the Fallen Angels attacking Christopher Knight and slamming him back and forth in a doorway, turning him into a bloody mess and killing him.

Now here is where the funniest thing happened. We were staying in a Holiday Inn type hotel and as I walked out of my room to head to the set these two ladies, still wearing their house coats, walked up to me. I said hello, and one of the ladies looked at me, they were both very excited about something, when the lady says "do you know Peter Brady?" I said "do you mean Christopher Knight?" The ladies giggled, they were so excited when I said 'yes, we've met." You would have thought they had just won the lottery. I looked at the women and said "as a matter of fact I am going to kill him right now." The ladies were over the moon, until... One of the women says "are you in the movie?" I looked her for a moment, and then said "there's a movie? "

If you could have seen their expressions change, it was priceless! I walked away without another word... I always wondered what their dinner time conversation was like...

I tried not to do it, I really did, but I couldn't help myself, the set up was way too good! (I can be a real jerk sometimes!)

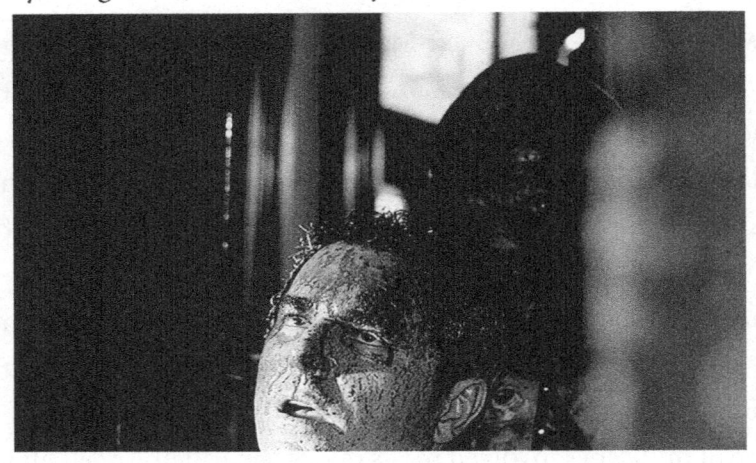

Christopher Knight in the front, me lurking

Chapter 23
Project Metalbeast

Kane Hodder hired me for a movie called Project Metalbeast, and I was to double Barry Bostwick.

I was supposed to get hit by this giant werewolf made out of metal, hence the name, and Kane wanted me to do something different and not land on any boxes, which is what we normally use to land in when we are up in the air, watch how many times you see that in a movie now! He really wanted me to go flying through the air to show how powerful the Metalbeast was, so we stood and looked around and tried to figure out what would look best when I spotted a steel roll up door.

We were in a water filtration plant and this door was super solid. I got back about five feet and ran and jumped up and hit my shoulder into it and it bounced me back about three feet, which gave me a great idea. I told Kane about my idea, I was going to run as fast as I could, then go off a Mini trampoline from about 8' to 10' away, go upside down, backwards, and hit the wall and fall onto the concrete with no pads underneath me.

Kane looked at me like I'm crazy and he says are you sure you want to do that? Now Kane doesn't realize that I already had a good idea that wall was going to kick me back several feet, and I could use that time to turn and I could come back and land right on my side where I had knee and elbow pads, and a good strong back pad on. I needed the back pad because I was going to hit that metal door going full speed directly upside down with my back.

I went in to hair and make up to get my hair to look like Barry Bostwick's, and got into my clothing for the stunt. I went back out to the set and I was waiting patiently for Kane to come out and I was stunned when I saw him... He comes out standing roughly 7 1/2 feet high in a werewolf costume made of metal, and it looked freaking awesome!

We set up for the for the stunt, we were going to do it in two parts, first part Kane will hit me with a huge right handed smash, and then we will cut, reset, and then do my off the wall (notice what I did there?) flying through the air stunt.

We line up for the first part of the stunt. I'm looking the monster right in the face and I had no idea that it was animatronic. As I'm standing there waiting for him to throw this huge right hand and rip off part of my face and send me flying, the monsters eyes turn to blood red, and the mouth opens, the teeth show and it growls bloody hell and I'm shocked! I think oh shit! Just for a second I thought that thing was real!

Just before we did the stunt I saw two younger guys standing around. We did the first part of the stunt where Kane hits me and I go backwards and land on the ground, and then I set up the mini tramp and was ready for the big stunt. I walked back about fifteen or twenty feet to get enough speed to get the height in the air I wanted, and I really need to be moving to get the distance I needed.

As I get ready I see Kane off to the side talking to the two young guys. I get set, the director yells action and I take off as fast as my chubby little legs can move, and I hit the mini tramp perfectly and went upside down exactly like I wanted to, hit exactly on my back like I wanted to, and then the major problem began. I was expecting to get a good bounce off the door so I could land on my side, but I hit the door so hard it went backwards!

I got absolutely none of the bounce back I was expecting and went straight down into the concrete on top of my head. I knew that my face would be towards camera so just as I landed I spun away from the camera so they couldn't tell that it wasn't Barry. I hear the director yell cut and Kane comes running over just as I get up. He looks at me with a real concerned look on his face and asks if I'm all right. I tell him I am ok, and then the director comes over to ask if I hurt myself, and of course I say no, that I am fine.

Just then I see the two young guys walking away, so I asked Kane who they were. He smiles and tells me that they wanted to become stuntmen, then he laughs and says and when they saw you hit the wall they changed their minds!

That was a wrap, so I headed to the Special Effects makeup department to get the makeup taken off, I had deep gashes in my face and neck where the Metalbeast had slashed me and sent me flying, and the white t-shirt I was wearing, it was mine, and I had to wear it home, was covered in blood. To my surprise, they had been wrapped for the day, and there was no one there to remove the makeup.

I had to drive home with the makeup on. It was very realistic looking, SFX makeup legend John Carl Buechler, , had applied it, so you know it looked phenomenal!

It was around 3am when I rolled into a 7-11 to get a six pack of Diet Coke so I could have something to drink for the ride home. I got the Coke and some candy and was standing in line when I realized the cashier had a very scared look on his face. He was staring at me like he might turn and run away, so I asked him what was wrong… he stumbled out the words "your face! "

I had forgotten about the makeup, and about the bloody t-shirt, so I can only imagine what the cashier must have thought! I was very tired, but not too tired to make light of the situation! I reached up and touched the slash marks, looked down at the bloody shirt, and then said 'oh, I have a cat" and walked out...

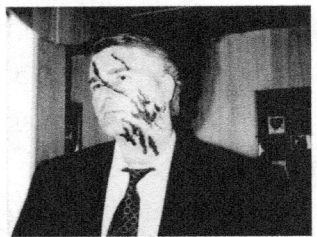

This past year I was a guest at the famous convention Scarefest and was walking to the restroom, just looking at the booths and all the horror and paranormal goodies on display when I looked up and I see Barry Bostwick! Now I had very briefly met him on Metalbeast, but being the friendly sort, I decided to introduce myself; after all, we had something in common!

I said "hi Barry, my name is Rick and we worked on a movie together". Now Metalbeast was over twenty years ago so I had no expectation that he would remember me, and he asked "what movie?" to which I said "Metalbeast". He looked at me for a minute, smiled and then said "you're the guy who went off the wall"! Now his reaction really made me happy, but what happened next was even better, he said he had a movie coming up where he might have some stunts, and did I have a card? I told him I would get him one for sure! I got swamped at the Hollywood Ghost Hunter booth when one of the workers from Scarefest came up to my table and said Barry sent me to get your card.

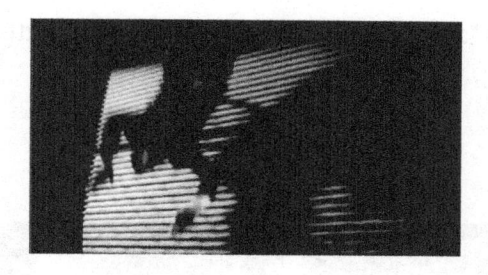

Thank you Barry, you made a guy feel appreciated

I Have Some of the Strangest Things Happen

Sometimes things happen that are so out there, you can't believe it just happened.

I was a guest at the Shooting Star Casino in Mahnomen, Minnesota for a paranormal convention along with Kane, representing the Hollywood Ghost Hunters. After the con closed for the day, I walked into the casino, and started chatting with some people I had met at the convention earlier that day, Eric and Lisa Heap, Karrie Grandbois, and Trinity Gruenberg.

We were all standing at one of those round table tops when a woman sitting at a table near me reached out and grabbed my hand and tried to pull me towards her. I held my ground; she was very strong, and also very drunk! I was trying to be a gentleman, but she wouldn't let go, no matter how many times or polite ways that I tried to tell her to turn me loose. Now you would think this is the strange part, but not even close! As I was trying to get her to let go of me, a lady I had met earlier named Treva Feezor came up behind me and bit me on the ass like a crocodile! I jumped, and my hand came loose from the lady. I asked Treva why she had chomped on me, and she said "I was trying to help you with the lady"... OK, there are about a million other ways that don't involve biting my ass, but I appreciated her extricating me.

Then Treva said "and besides, you have a biteable butt." Sometimes my life is… unusual?

Me at work

Love in the Time of Monsters 　　Hatchet 2

The Patriot 　　The Devil's Rejects

Fallen Angels 　　J Edgar 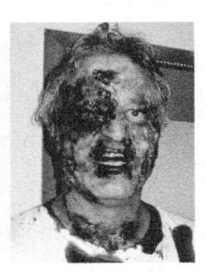　　Born

Chapter 24
The Oman House

I first became aware of the Oman House after seeing it on an episode of Ghost Hunters, and was really interested in the EVPs that the team and guest Chris Fleming had gotten.

Many of you may have seen David's house on Ghost Adventures, as well as many other shows.I started doing research on how to contact the owner of the house, David Oman. The house is named after him, not the movie the Omen. I was finally able to track him down and he agreed to let us do a hunt there. One of the first things you notice about David Oman is that he is a pretty nice guy, and very connected to the spirits in his house, and he will talk to them as he walks around the house. I believe he invites them in by being so open to them, which I think is a good thing..

He started to take us into a short hallway towards a bathroom. I instantly stopped because I felt a huge field of energy outside the bathroom and told David. He replied that several psychics, most notably James Van Praagh had said there was a vortex in the bathroom; I told him I thought it was about fifteen outside of it.

The upper level of the house has the famous aquarium room, which is where the figurines get knocked over without anyone touching them, it has happened while we have been there, and I have been there many times. To the right if you are standing in the middle of the house and looking back to the front door is the hallway to the bathroom, and if you continue to the right is the kitchen.

Robert Pendergraft took a series of pictures starting at the aquarium room, then towards the bathroom hallway, then the last picture of the kitchen. The first picture, the aquarium room is clear as a bell, the second, and the hallway where I said I felt the energy was all orange, and the third picture in the series was also totally clear. He took these one after the other, so the middle picture coming out all orange haze while the pictures he took before and after is very interesting for sure.

David next took us to the second level where his office is, his bedroom is also on that floor, and I have to say that hallway is one of the most active places I have ever seen.

One of the very first times I walked down that hallway, the overhead lighting went berserk, the recessed lights all started lighting up randomly, we have it on tape, and David Oman told us that the lights couldn't possibly be flashing out of sequence and independently, as they were all on one electrical line. And then the smoke alarm went off! OK, this house is definitely getting my attention.

On one occasion we were doing a Frank's Box session with Christopher Moon on the lowest level when we heard very loud walking above us, loud enough that I suspected someone was up there playing a joke. Robert was standing next to the spiral staircase and instantly went up to check. He had just come back down the stairs when it sounded like someone stomping along the length of the hallway above us, again he went up, this time I followed him, and while he checked the second floor, I continued up to the top floor. Neither of us found anybody.

I put a night vision camera on the floor of the second floor hallway; I like to set it on the ground so you get the entire view, and so that nothing could be missed by putting it on a tripod. When I was reviewing the footage I was startled to find a transparent figure go flashing by the camera. Now the thing you have to know is we were all outside at the time, no one was in the house. I get a real kick from the responses I get when I show people that footage, most people get startled when the image streaks by… that wasn't the only image that I caught, as I continued to review the footage I saw what looks like a baton shaped object, some say it could be a hatchet or tomahawk, transparent of course, but easily visible come out from the left side wall, turn in midair and vanish. That hallway has some very strong activity; this is the same hallway that we heard all the footsteps in.

I have also had many experiences on the bottom floor. On the same day Chris Moon was doing the Frank's Box, both Robert and I heard something outside, so we opened the door to the outside, and there was a stairway made of cement slabs that ran from the first floor, down to the landing I was standing on, and then down another flight and turned at the bottom around the corner. I stayed on the landing while Robert went down to see what had made the noise. It was very quiet outside, the stairs had dry leaves on them, and I heard the crunching of leaves coming down from the top of the stars toward me. I turned to look to see who it was; it was loud enough I thought one of our team was walking down the stairs. Surprise! No one was there, but the footsteps kept coming towards me… I stood there as the sound of crunching leaves came towards me step by step, finally stopping on the stair above me. I realized if this was indeed was a spirit trying to get my attention, and the footsteps crunching the leaves coming down the stairs right at me certainly got my attention, I realized that we were probably standing face to face. I did the only thing I could think of and said "hi."

I had barely said hi when I heard the leaves crunching again, this time it was Robert coming back up the stairs, and he said he didn't find anything that could've have made the noise. I am very sure that I found what caused it!

On another hunt at David's house, Louis Horowitz and I were on the bottom floor, and Louis had just sat down on the sofa, and I had been packing up my equipment and had just closed the case and set it on the floor. I looked over towards Louis and couldn't believe what I was seeing. David's house had a window that had vinyl vertical blinds, and he had two or three extra hanging over the top, similar to how you would hang a towel over the shower door. I was watching the extra vertical blinds swinging back and forth like a metronome, and as Louis had passed by them to sit down, I figured he probably bumped into them, causing them to move back and forth, but I was wrong. I asked him if he had bumped into them, and he said no, but as I looked, I realized the blinds were hanging over the top, and were too high for him to have bumped into. All of a sudden they sped up; I was thinking the window was open and the wind was blowing them, causing them to move. Wrong again… They were still moving as I walked towards them, then they suddenly stopped. I looked behind the blinds, the window was not open, and Louis and I looked for air conditioning vents, or anything that might have caused the movement, but couldn't find anything…

Ghosts Believe in Me

Why do things always get interesting as soon as you put the equipment away?

There have been many other instances that have happened at David's house, he has been nice enough to let me come up there several times, but one of the things that stand out to me was Chris Moon's Frank's Box session. For those who don't know what a Frank's Box is, it is also called The Telephone of the Dead, and is used to communicate with spirits, much the way a Spirit Box works, only on steroids. It also has the distinction of having been invented by Thomas Edison.

Chris Moon had come out from Colorado to interview us for his magazine, Haunted Times, and he brought along a Frank's Box. I had never seen one, because the one's made by Frank Sumption are very rare, so I was anxious to see how it worked. He set it up and we all crowded around as Chris started.

During the session we heard the word Kane come through, and later in the session we heard "help me ", but the real highlight of the session came at the very end, and I think most of the group wasn't aware of what was going on. Let me fill you in a bit on why this was so compelling. Almost the entire group was there, I think twelve us all together, and we had well-known actors, stuntmen, directors, special effects guys, and writers, all who would be very easy to get information on if you were trying to fake something. I only say that to show you why this was really something if you knew the story behind it, which I did.

This is in no way a suggestion that Chris would fake something in the first place, I've known Chris Moon for a long time and he has a sterling reputation and is a man of great integrity, this was only said to show you why the story was so cool. If someone had wanted to try and fool us, they would have used Kane, R.a., or any of the other members it would have easy to get information about... All our members are famous in their own right, except one, and finding info about him would be very hard, most likely impossible. I am speaking about my friend Louis Horowitz, who was working at Fox at the time, so I was very surprised when Chris told Louis someone named Rose wanted to talk to him. Louis had told me he had gotten into ghost hunting because the night his grandmother Rose died, he had gotten up to get a drink of water in the kitchen late at night, and his grandmother was standing there. Louis always thought she had come to say goodbye to him, they were very close.

When I heard Chris tell Louis that someone named Rose wanted to talk to him he was totally stunned. He said "is this my bubby" and the reply was "yes". Chris had another surprise for Louis when he said "do you know someone named Irene?" I saw the look on Louis' face; I thought he was going to lose it right there, when he replied "that's my other bubby!"

Louis asked if they were in heaven together when the response was a clear "where else would we be?" They seemed to have moved on, but I was happy my friend had such a profound experience. I told you Christopher Moon is the real deal! I have had many paranormal experiences at the Oman House, but that one will stand out.

Scarefest!

I was so excited when Kane told me I had been invited to Scarefest in Lexington Kentucky. Scarefest is one of the best horror and paranormal conventions in the country, so I was very proud to have been invited to help represent the Hollywood Ghost Hunters. Kane, R.a. and Steve Nappe, another member, would all be there.

I couldn't believe how many people came to my table! I saw celebrities everywhere, many that I had worked with on different films, as well as some of the most recognizable people from TV and movies.

Kristin and Nicole   Deb and Kathy   Kimberly

My booth was right next to the Mountain Monsters TV show, and really had great time talking to Buck… They were all really great guys! I had to give Buck one of our team hats… And Kat Hobson from Fate Magazine Radio too!

Kat   Buck

There Must Be Another Rick McCallum!

The highlight of The Scarefest was getting to meet my crush in person, the founder of the Hollywood Ghost Hunters, Rick McCallum. I'd seen him on an episode of Ghost Adventures years ago and was enthralled.

I totally fan-girled out and couldn't talk when I first saw him, but then a funny thing happened. Rick turned out to be an incredibly gracious, warm, and salt-of-the-earth person. His charm and wit melted my nerves and I ended up having an amazing talk with him too.

Do I still have a bit of a crush? Of course! But even more than that I have the utmost and respect and admiration for him because he's a class act all the way. Even though he lives and works in Hollywood, he's not full of himself. He's humble, generous, and doesn't take himself too seriously. That was not only unexpected but very refreshing. (Because I've met people with not even a tenth of his credentials who are so full of themselves it's disgusting.

So, yeah. Rick was a surprise and a great example.) Courtney Mroch, Author: The Ghost of Laurie Floyd

(She only likes me because her skeleton does!)

Skelly and Rick

Chapter 25
Sometimes there is Much More to Find

Many years ago I was contacted to ghost hunt a place in Los Angeles that was frequented by a very famous person that I am not allowed to disclose. Trust me he was world famous, probably the most famous person in the world in his time.

There were many reports of paranormal happenings, so I grabbed Robert Pendergraft, a well-known SFX artist who among many things did the amazing make up on Kane Hodder in the Hatchet movies, and Ed Ackerman, who costarred in Hatchet 2 and is very well known as one of the Visigoths in The Capital One commercials, who are both members of The Hollywood Ghost Hunters and we headed out.

When we arrived we were shown around the grounds and the home, which was big and very beautiful, and we were told the history of the place, that there used to be a quartz mine there which immediately caught our interest as quartz is believed to hold energy and can make spirit interaction ramp up, and the most interesting piece of history being a tunnel that went under the busy street to another house that several movie stars had owned at different times. They would walk through the tunnel to visit each other and none of the neighbors knew of the tunnel. Unfortunately the tunnel had been closed and filled in. We split up, Ed and I went in the house while Robert and his friend Duke took the outside, which featured hills, terraces and staircases and was very large for a home in the Hollywood Hills.

We investigated most of the house when we finally went to the bottom floor, and things got very interesting! We walked into a bedroom and we both saw a very large shadow go across the wall. Trying to debunk it, we went back and forth through the doorway several times but couldn't make any shadow at all...

The room consisted of two beds and a small sofa against the wall, then a bathroom on the far side. I set the K2 meter and the voice recorder on the bed closet to the bathroom, and sat on the sofa about 10 feet away.

Ed picked up the K2 meter and started into the bathroom saying he wanted to get a base reading. Ed had no sooner walked into the room than the meter started reacting, so I joined him to see what was going on.

We started asking if this was the famous person (we obviously used his name) with no response, so we decided to call out names of people we knew had been there. Once again we started with him, then his wife, and then the owner of the house with no response when Ed remembered about the quartz mine. He asked if he was a miner... Bingo! The K2 lit up with all 5 lights.

Now when I investigate I always ask twice if I get a response so we went through the names again, nothing till we got to the miner, then once again all 5 lights!

As we started trying to communicate we weren't getting any response so I asked if it wanted us to leave, instantly all 5 lights again. I decided to try and test it, so I asked if it wanted us to stay... nothing... so I said if you light this up again we'll leave... bam, instant 5 lights! Ed looked at me and said "what do we do now?" I smiled and said "we go, it's his house".

Ghosts Believe in Me

We walked into the next room to get the voice recorder and started to talk about being thrown out and just then all 5 lights again… I said "do it again and we are out of here". Bam, all 5! Keeping our word, we left, truly the only time a spirit had thrown me out of somewhere, but its intent was unmistakable!

A few days later I was reviewing the voice recorder, and when it got to the bedroom you can hear Ed pick up the K2 from the bed and head to the bathroom, saying "I'm going to get a base reading", and that was followed about 4 seconds later by a very clear, very aggressive sounding "NO!" right into the microphone.

OK, why the title for this piece? I was outside Rosslyn Castle on the bridge at about 1 in the morning when Gary Hughill, a ghost hunter from England asked if I ever got any EVP's, so I played him the one with the "NO!"

He looked at me and said what a great catch that was, and I replied "yeah the NO is pretty strong!" What he said next really took me by surprise… He said "no mate, what it says before that". Huh? What? I had heard that EVP probably 100 times from playing it for people and hadn't heard anything besides NO!

He tells me there are 4 words before the NO! We listen very carefully; it was like a scene out of a movie, 2 guys on a bridge next to a castle in the middle of the night. I cranked up the volume and sure enough, it is faint, but I do hear the cadence of 4 words, then NO!

I couldn't really tell what the words were so Gary volunteered to tell me. Alright, what does it say? He responded "it says "get back here punk, then NO!" As soon as I got back to my room I took out my portable speaker, cranked up the volume, and sure enough, there it was! So sometimes, there is more than you think! Put on the headphones, crank up the volume!

Chapter 26
The Graber Olive House, Home and Family TV Halloween Ghost Hunt

My first visit to the Graber Olive House in Ontario, California was several years ago, when my friend Scott Gruenwald (Paranormal Paparazzi) invited our group out for his paranormal get together, called Stu Con. We had been to other Stu Cons, the ones at Linda Vista Hospital, and had a blast, always fun to meet new people, and although it was fifty miles away, which meant I would have to drive for an hour each way, which was fine, but it also meant I had to listen to Ra Mihailoff, also known as Leatherface from Texas Chainsaw Massacre 3..even that didn't stop me!

As we went through this very nice neighborhood of homes, we spotted it, and pulled over and parked.. About a block away, because people were already there, it is always well attended.

We walked up to the event, and it was hopping! Scott always makes sure it's entertaining, I mean, really, where else can you find a full grown man in a tutu being shot by paintball guns? True story, he does it every year. That boy has issues, I think... BTW, Mr. Gruenwald, do another Stu Con!

The Graber Olive House is a house, and next to it, an olive processing plant, owned by Cliff Graber, who I've come to know, and is a genuinely really good man, who gave us the tour of the place. During the day it is a quaint house up front, and a rustic type of factory, it has an old loft area that resembles a barn, which has a great look, and several rooms of vats, lots of vats for the olives. It doesn't have a hint of being haunted at all. That changes quickly when it gets dark...

I was running around like a kid in a candy store, listened to a fascinating talk by Ben Hansen, went over and chatted with Britt Griffith from Ghost Hunters, and then I stopped by Mike Murray's booth, P-Tec, who builds some really excellent equipment. Of course I had to buy some infrared lights (glad I did, they work much better than the Sony light I have), also picked up a device that will light up and emit an alarm when it detects footsteps, and a piece of equipment that attaches to your voice recorder, and has lights that will tell you when it hears a sound, great for checking EVP's!

R.a. Mihailoff was over regaling Leatherface fans, letting them bask in the mega wattage of his superstardom.

We met some great people, ate some of the best tacos ever, and you will always have a good time when Scott Gruenwald is around. I also really enjoyed the speeches, the booths were cool too. They had an auction, and I bought more lights from Mike Murray and P-Tec, yeah, what can I say, they are good lights!

I also met the guys from the group Darklands Paranormal, Marco Santucci and Scott Ault, who run the ghost hunts at Graber, which would come in handy.

I was asked to take Debbie Matenopolous on a hunt for a Halloween bit on the Home and Family TV show, and I thought the Graber Olive House would be perfect. Debbie was on the View before Home and Family, so I was really looking forward to taking her along. I thought the location would look great in the dark, rustic and creepy enough for TV, and would probably get some good reactions from Debbie, as it was her first hunt.

Ghosts Believe in Me

Rick, R.a. and Ed Ackerman on Hatchet 2

Apparently ghosts can become enamored of some people, and I think a spirit had the hots for Debbie. We had the K2 out, and it wouldn't go off for us, but if Debbie talked, it would respond, three to five light responses! Debbie was getting a big kick out of this, and was playing along, which got even more activity...

Criminy sakes you two, get a room! As we went along, it responded five lights to her, and she said "oh, I love you! Will you come home with me?" Oh no! Old Rick will not stand by quietly for that one! I told her that if you invite a spirit to go with you, sometimes it will... I then said forcefully "you understand that you can't go with Debbie, this is your place, and you have to stay here"? Evidently the spirit understood, we got a five light response... I don't know who the spirit is, but Cliff Graber thought it might be a former worker there, and it responded when Cliff asked if it was him, but I think I would've liked him...

Marco Santucci and Scott Ault were also there asking questions, and we got a lot of activity, and like I said, it may look kind of serene in the daytime, but it can surprise you at night.

It was starting to get late, so we headed down to the vat room, a very eerie looking place in the dark, row after row of vats, in a room of dark wood. Ed Ackerman, the other HGH member had been filming, so he and I switched places, I filmed while he worked with Debbie... Ed is a big dude, very funny guy, he plays one of the Visigoths on the Capitol One commercials, and he also costarred in Hatchet 2, so he is good on camera, and he is always a good addition to a hunt.

Ed started showing Debbie around, and answering her questions, as I filmed the vat room... The Home and Family crew were filming them, and as I swept the camera across the room, a white shape came up from the vats and darted across the screen... we stopped filming, rewound the camera, and watched the playback, you can see a small white transparent shape dart up from the floor. Ed, Debbie and I tried to recreate it, Cliff had a small flashlight, but he and everyone else were in the other room, with a wall between where they were, and where I was filming. We had Cliff shine his light into the room several times, but could barely see the light at all, and the angle was all wrong for him to have been able to cause it... As always, we let you decide what you think it may be...

I have to say, it was a great time, Cliff gave us all a box of olives, which was very kind, and may I say delicious?! Thank you Cliff! Thanks to Scott Ault and Marco Santucci of Darklands Paranormal for the location hook up, to Debbie Matenopoulous, who is an absolute sweetheart, and to Home and Family for having us on their show.

Rick and Debbie Matenopolous

Chapter 27
The Pioneer Saloon

I was invited to join a ghost hunt at the famous Pioneer Saloon in Good Springs Nevada, by Jill Allen Padovese of Pioneer Saloon Investigators, also known by her wonderful nickname Jilly Beans, and had been driving down from Las Vegas, listening to music and feeling excited about getting to explore such an iconic location.

I turned off the highway onto a dark, lonely two way road, you know, the kind of road they use in horror movies and drove seven miles, all the time thinking that if the Pioneer Saloon is at the end of this road it must haunted. I had no idea how right I was.

As I drove over the top of the hill, I could see below me the Pioneer Saloon. It truly was a sight to see, it was almost like going back in time. As I pulled in front and parked, I was impressed by the authentic look of the building. I walked to the left side of the building into the Good Springs general store, where I met the Lead Investigator, Jill Allen Padovese. The best way to describe her is as a human tornado, with an infectious laugh that you can feel all the way down to your toes. I knew I would enjoy myself with her showing me around.

We sat down in a long bar waiting for the rest of the members to appear, and talked about some of the occurrences that happened there...

History of the saloon

The Saloon is probably most famous due to a tragedy that occurred on a mountaintop nearby. The famous actress Carole Lombard was killed in a plane crash, and Clark Gable sat quietly at the bar as they tried to recover his wife's body. Some claim Carole still visits the bar.

The Clark Gable room

The haunted lockdown events originally started late in 2013 after the airing of the Ghost Adventures episode featuring the 100+ year old saloon and town. The proprietor, Noel Sheckells saw an opportunity to allow the general public to experience the same paranormal event as Zak, Nick and Aaron did when they were "locked" into the saloon for an overnight investigation.

He also had the idea of all the proceeds to be donated back to the town of Good Springs as a charitable deed and to keep a small town up of a little over 200 residents alive. I was lucky enough to meet Noel and some of his family who work there, and every one of them is as nice as you could ask for, and they make you feel welcome from the minute you walk in the door.

All of what happened next was captured on audio and video

Jill then took us to the back room, where there were two round tables, and I sat in the very spot where a man had been shot to death cheating at cards. Even as I sat down I had a very funny feeling that there were spirits near me, and I was to find out very quickly that I was correct.

As we sat down, the guests, the investigators and I all set out our equipment, there were several voice recorders, and I had in front of me a K2 meter and the girl next to me also set hers in front of me; because she was sitting in the curve of the table, and the only place she could set hers was directly next to mine. Jill had been telling us more of the history and after about 5 minutes both of the K 2 meters in front of me went off with all 10 lights flashing, and they continued to go full blast for about ten seconds, when they instantly stopped.

We were all are chatting, and after a short time once again all 10 lights started flashing in front of me.

I have been ghost hunting for over thirty years and what happened next has never happened to me before.

I instantly became incredibly sick to my stomach, so much so that I thought I was going to be sick right then and there. I felt my body begin to tense up, and an intensely cold feeling went through my entire body. Jill, looking at the K2 meter going off says I think the spirits really like you. I replied I'm not so sure they do. Right at this moment the video captures a voice, a woman's voice saying "we do". Immediately following that you can hear "Rick" being called out, which we heard with our own ears at the time. Jill takes a good look at me and says" what's wrong"? I asked Jill to feel my forehead and as she does she says "oh my God you're as cold as ice". The girl sitting next to me then reaches over and touches my left forearm and she says the same thing.

I am feeling so sick I get up and go outside to try and catch some fresh air, and as I walk about a foot and a half behind another girl that is sitting facing away from me she says" I can feel how cold he is from here". I make it outside as the group continues to investigate. In the past I have been touched by spirits and on occasion I have felt a cold spot develop where I felt a touch, this however is my entire body, so all I can surmise is that I'm being touched by multiple entities.

I lean against the rail trying to compose myself, I haven't been this sick for a long time, and after about 10 minutes Jill comes out to check on me. We talk for a few minutes, and I feel much better and decide to go back inside and resume the hunt. As soon as we walk in the door I feel like I've been hit by a tsunami of sickness, and the ice cold feeling instantly returns. There is no way that I can continue the investigation, as I fear that I will ruin it for everyone, and I decide that it is best that I leave.

The rest of the investigators were still at the tables and turned around, looking to see if I was all right, when I told them that I thought it was best that I left for the evening, and as I turned to leave there was a voice captured, an EVP, not an actual voice you can hear at the time which said" turn Rick back". For some reason I stopped and turned back to them to say my goodbyes and once again turned to leave when another voice says this time a man's voice" release him" as I was walking away.

The fresh air made me feel a little bit better, clearing my head, but I was still incredibly sick to my stomach and during the drive back to Las Vegas there were many times when I almost pulled off the road to get sick. I finally reached my evil stepmothers house where I was staying, and the rest of the night wasn't great, but when the morning rolled around I felt a lot better.

Jill called me later that week and asked how I was feeling, and then told me something that really caught my interest.

It appears that on two more ocassisions during their investigation that people heard my name called out. I was later to find out that it happened again the following day. It seems like something really wanted my attention, I just wish it could find a better way of showing it!

Ara and Darrell Harris, Jill Allen Padovese, Jennifer Fargnoli, Linda Masanimptewa

Chapter 28
The Buffalo Central Terminal

I was leading a ghost hunt, at the Buffalo Central Terminal along with Jack Kenna who you have probably seen on Haunted Case Files. We also had with us Chris Gurnett, a young guy who is an expert on the paranormal happenings of the Terminal.

The first area we went was a lobby type area with a staircase right up the middle, with very old time train station décor. We had only been there a few minutes when the fun started…

People were milling around, moving about the location, so I pulled out my tablet and connected my Flir thermal imager. I scanned the room, the people showed up as an array white, yellow degrees, while colder images shows up light blue, dark purple, I have not seen a totally black heat signature yet.

I was scanning the room when I noticed a light blue figure standing in the back near the stairway, a human shape beyond question! I called everybody together and we all saw it clear as possible. Jack Kenna called out for it to move, and it took three steps to the right and stopped.

Everybody was looking at it move, stunned by what they were seeing… To confirm it was actually responding I called out for it to do something and let us know it was an actual spirit… I couldn't believe it when it walked three steps away from the stairs, raised its right arm and disappeared, and all the people had been crowding around the thermal image on the tablet, and they had seen it for themselves.

This would be a classic Class A piece of evidence, so I hit the play button on the tablet, and was extremely disappointed to say the least when we saw that the video had frozen before all this had happened, it would show you the images on screen but some glitch in the tablet would only record a very short clip. Fortunately quite a few people could verify what we saw. I believe Chris saw it, as well as Jessica Leigh, who was my henchperson for the convention. I know they are called handlers, but my people are henchpersons! (Isn't that right Barbara Maggard from Scarefest?)

> I have to say it is a class A thermal shot. Conducting tours and ghost hunts over the years I have never seen as good a thermal image from there that was on one of my tours.
>
> Chris Gurnett

After such an amazing scene at the Trolley Lobby, we were pretty excited, but I didn't expect anything more that could compete with what we had just seen, which was awesome! Boy was I wrong!

We made our way to an upper floor, which was a long hallway with doors on the side. There was a table stretched across the hallway like a barrier, which we all used to put our equipment on. Several of the guests started saying they were seeing a shadow peek its head out into hallway from one of the rooms on the side.

I believe Ghost Hunters caught something coming out as well on their TV show. Jack decided to enter the rooms on the left side of the hallway to see if he could stir up some activity, and we all watched the hallway with the thermal imager.

It wasn't very long when the thermal imager picked up what looked like Jack... then another figure followed right behind him! I thought it might be a homeless person, and I yelled "Jack, there is someone behind you!" I instantly went around the table to go help Jack just in case it was someone who might have bad intentions... I'll let Jack finish the story...

> I entered the room through the doorway next to me and Rick, walked to the center of the room, and then told Rick and the group that I was beginning to make my way down the center of the room. I could hear Rick and the group talking the whole time, as I approached the half way mark of the room, and had just passed a closed door to my right that was an entrance to the hallway, I heard Rick and group yell to me. Rick informed that something had just come out behind me into the hallway as they saw it on his thermal imager! At first I thought he meant that a figure had come out into the hallway through the closed door that I had just passed, so I yelled back to him about that door being closed, and he said "No, a figure actually followed you out into the hallway!" I stood there for a moment dumbfounded. It was obvious now that Rick and the group thought I had just walked out into the hallway! I told them that was not possible as I was still standing in the middle of the room! I was not in the hallway! I could hear them all saying things like "What?", "No, you just came out into the hallway." and

"Jack stop kidding around, we all just saw you on the thermal walk into the hallway and something came out right behind you!" It was then that I insisted that I was still in the room and had not come out; I was still working my way down inside the room! It was then that they came down the hallway to where they heard me and I met them all at the next open doorway to the hall. They were shocked. They couldn't believe that I had not left the room. I had Rick replay the footage for me, and in it you could see a figure that looked kind of like me step into the hallway, followed by another and then the image froze, so there was no way to see where the figures had gone to after entering the hallway. Now, the next interesting thing is that the figures did come out of the door that was shut! We went over to that door and tried to open it, we couldn't. It seemed to be locked, and there was no glass in the window that was in it, so that ruled out a possible thermal reflection, but again we saw on the footage that the figures stepped out into the hallway through a locked door. Now I may be able to do a lot of things, but I am not capable of being in two places at once and I am not able to walk through locked doors as if they aren't there! This just blew our minds! Neither Rick, nor I, or anyone of the few paranormal investigators that were with us that night had ever seen anything like that before in all of our years investigating.

Chapter 29
Rosslyn Forest, Scotland

I was staying across the street from Rosslyn Chapel, made famous by the DaVinci Code, and thought was that the Knights Templar may have brought the Holy Grail and the Ark of the Covenant to hide here. I have ghost hunted all around the forest, by the castle and the three cemeteries, and have walked eight miles through the forest many times, so I have a pretty good idea about the area, and was looking for somewhere else to hunt, it had to be within walking distance, which if you just read above I can walk some distance pretty easily.

I had been shown a marker about a mile away commemorating the Battle of Rosslyn in 1303.

The battle took place in the forest and fields farther down the street, in the opposite direction from the Chapel. 8,000 Scots took on 30,000 English troops and sent them running. It is one of the first battles that Wallace was in, and I thought it would be a great place to go to late at night and to walk through the battle site with my thermal imager and my other usual equipment. I decided to check the place out during the day so I had my bearings when it was dark.

I walked about a mile till I came to the monument and noticed a path into the woods, which I set out on. I had walked maybe a mile and a half, looking for the perfect place to ghost hunt that night. As I came to a small hill on the path, I started down it not realizing it was muddy underneath the top layer.

As I put my left foot down it slipped and as I was on an incline my foot went flying up in the air, kicking me backwards. My right foot got caught behind me with my foot facing the ground and I took a very hard fall, something I'm used to, but with my foot stuck I fell directly onto my knee with all my weight and my leg completely slammed shut at the knee as I fell on top of it.

I slid down the hill with my foot caught behind me and I could feel the muscles around my knee and thigh being stretched way too far. The pain was incredible, but I deal with pain pretty well, being in the stunt business for as long as I have you get used to it, but this was a serious injury.

I had to roll to my left side to free my leg and physically had to reach behind me to grab it and straighten it out in front of me... I sat there in the mud for about five minutes waiting for the leg to quit spasming. I carefully got to my feet and looked at the muddy hill I just fell down and realized there was no way I could get back up it, it was too slippery and I knew my right leg wouldn't let me anyway.

I looked around and saw a flat path heading the other direction; I set off even though I had no idea where it would lead me. I limped badly for two and a half miles till I came to a farm. There were two metal cattle gates I had to climb over, not easy with a messed up leg and muddy shoes, but I made it over and started walking to the farm, as I could see the barns a couple of hundred yards away.

I made my way to a street with some houses on it, and I was looking for someone to tell me where I was, and I saw a man at his kitchen sink, so I called out to him. He looked out at me, sees me covered in mud and limping badly and I was afraid he would think I was the Walking Dead!

I asked him if this road would take me to where I could catch a bus back to Roslin, and he said yes but it wasn't close. I thanked him and started limping down the street.

I had only gone maybe fifty yards when he pulls up next to me and says get in. I thanked him for the offer but told him I didn't want to get his car dirty. He just chuckled and said I work on a farm, get in. I happily did and he drove me to my hotel, and he even turned the car around so I could get out closer to the door. I thanked him profusely as he headed off and made my way into the hotel, where a few of the girls who worked there saw me and asked if I needed an ambulance.

I thanked them but said no and started up the stairs with them both right behind making sure I would make it.

I never felt so good to get into a shower in my life.

Why did I write this? Because I needed to say to Jamie Cameron of Lang Hill Farms, and the people at the Chapel Cross Inn, you are some amazing people and truly Angels on Earth! Update: As I write this it has been over a year since I fell, and it is still hard to get up and down the stairs…

I made it back to Roslin the next year, still wanting to check out the battlefields where 38,000 English and Scottish fought in what is considered the bloodiest battle between the two countries.

I called Jamie Cameron and we made plans to check out the fields, which are right outside his house. I went to his house at 10 PM, and met his lovely wife Christine, and their two children, Charlie and Katie. What a nice family they are!

Jamie and I spent the next several hours out in the fields, where we witnessed an awesome moonrise. Being out in those dark, moonlit fields had a very mystical feel; you could see the outlines of the darkened buildings and fences as the moon crept higher in the sky. I had a thermal imager that I was sweeping the fields with, and Jamie had the night vision camera and the K2 meter. We walked through the fields, and they had the most serene feel to them, I was very happy just being out in such a gorgeous evening. We didn't get even a single bit of activity that night, which some people might say was a waste of time, but for me it was just the opposite.

Knowing that all those brave men that fought to the death in those fields 700 years had gone to their reward left me with a very peaceful feeling, and of a night well spent.

Ghosts Believe in Me

Sometimes the best evidence is no evidence at all. RIP gentlemen…

Chapter 30
Hunting with Scottish Paranormal

I was standing outside in front of the Montague Guest House, where I was staying waiting for the guys from Scottish Paranormal to pick me up. A few days earlier I had taken a very hard fall down a hill in Rosslyn Forest and messed up my right knee, it was so bad I could barely walk on it.

I knew I was being taken on an all day tour and I knew there would be A LOT of walking, so I had some trepidation about meeting them, not sure how they would react to my slow limping way of getting around. I had no intention of not going, and was determined to have a good time and to try to keep up with them. That was totally put at ease when I met them in person. As the guys from Scottish Paranormal arrived we made our introductions and I was really happy to meet them and it felt like we'd been friends forever.

Ally Reid, Gregor Stewart, Ryan O'Neill

Now all of them are very well known paranormal investigators, Greg and Ryan are both published authors on the paranormal and Ally Reid has one of the best coffee shops in all of Scotland, as well as a cookbook with a paranormal theme (The Rick McCallum Burger is in it!) All three are very highly thought of paranormal investigators. I was really looking forward to the adventure, but definitely not the walking.

We headed out through the town where I saw many of the highlights that St. Andrews has to offer, and it is a beautiful place, and not only the golf course, which is of course the oldest and most famous in the world. And the coastline is absolutely stunning!

I really enjoyed when we got up to St. Andrews University because in my research of my ancestors I had found out that Zachary McCallum was a very famous swordsman who in a battle killed 7 men in a row before he was killed from behind with a scythe, and was the only man to ever beat Alastair the Devastator in single combat.

He had actually matriculated at St. Andrews University.

I couldn't envision myself going to school there just because the place is so beautiful, still in a very old time stately way.

My next surprise was one we got up to St. Andrew's cathedral which had been the site of many battles and most of it had been destroyed but what is still remaining is very historical and beautiful in its own way. It is also a graveyard where I saw the resting places of Young and Old Tom Morris, the famous father and son who dominated the British Open golf tournament for years.

I had another surprise as Gregor's son Kyle is actually one of the tour guides there and he took us through the entire place which is nothing short of fantastic. The views along the coastline are worth a visit by themselves but the history of the buildings, and all the supernatural and paranormal reports from the place give it a great air in a spooky sort of way... Of course the graveyard has many sightings of apparitions, and one of the buildings was found to have multiple bodies in it, including a woman wearing a long white dress.

Why is the dress always white? Kyle is also a very well-known photographer and artist and I was so pleased that he gave me two of his pictures as a present when I was leaving. The Scottish people are the friendliest and most giving people that I've ever come across and I certainly have to put these guys in the same group.

Kyle, thank you for the great tour!

Chapter 31
Balgonie Castle

We headed out towards Balgonie Castle which ended up being a fair drive through some gorgeous countryside and when we finally pulled up in front of the castle it was everything that you would expect.

I instantly fell in love with the place but I had a much bigger surprise coming when I got inside. I got to meet the Lord of the castle, a man in his mid-eighties who looks exactly like a Lord of the castle should, with the kilt, and the long Gray beard and hair, he looked every bit like he came from central casting.

The Laird and his faithful friend Alfie

He had this dog that went everywhere with him so you could not have gotten a better flavor of the atmosphere of the castle and the occupants.

He turned out to be an extraordinary artisan who not only excelled in leatherwork; he also carved the doors of this castle, as well as many beautiful paintings throughout the castle.

Every single thing he showed me was world class! One thing that I'll always treasure and I mean that as seriously as I can, was that the Laird of the manor had seen that I'd been limping all over the place and asked me if I could climb three flights of stairs. I said sure as long as there's a railing I'm good to go.

He then invited us up to his private residence and I understand he doesn't do that very often…

Everything he told me was just fascinating; I could have stayed there and talked to him all night! It was a pleasure and honor to meet such a nice, talented and accomplished man! As I made way up the three flights of stairs Ally Reid leaned over and told me that this is the first time that they were going up there too. So I felt extra honored that he asked me to go. Once we got up there it was an amazing sight! It had the old stone walls, and it had these really dark huge rafters brown rafters that had names painted on the bottom of them, turns out that they were the family crests of 31 other families that previously had been Lairds of the castle. They were painted on what looked similar to

Shields, and had hung them into the ceiling and all of them painted by the Laird himself!

Inside was a huge stone fireplace probably 6' across by 4-5' high, it was absolutely gigantic, all around the place were these old worn brown leather chairs and a sofa which just made the place look like a piece of history. I could have stayed up there the whole time!

We headed downstairs to begin the ghost hunt where we first entered sort of a waiting area, grabbed up all the gear and headed into the chapel. What a sight to see! Just the feeling of walking in there, you could feel the history wash over you, all I could do was just stand there looking at everything. We set up the equipment, I had only brought a few things as they had told me they had quite a bit of equipment, and as they were putting it around different areas I decided I would try the K2 meter.

Gregor had told me the story of Mary Sibbald, who they think is actually a resident spirit at Balgonie Castle so I started asking if this was Mary. I started getting 5 light responses to all of my questions and finally had to call Gregor over because I didn't know enough of the story of Mary to ask her anything. As soon as he came over the lights stopped completely. I decided it was her way of saying hello to me.

The entrance to the Chapel **The Chapel**

As Ryan O'Neill, Ally Reid and I (Gregor Stewart) turned into Murray Park in St Andrews to meet Rick McCallum of Hollywood Ghost Hunters outside his hotel, there was a mix of excitement and apprehension! Excitement to finally meet the man we had seen on TV, read about and spoke to on many occasions, and apprehension for the same reason! Yet that apprehension proved to be unjust when we finally met Rick, who instantly made us feel at ease before the joking began, when he pointed out that the bold capital letters of the text 'Scottish Paranormal Investigation Team' printed across the back of our T-Shirts spelled 'SPIT'!

We took Rick on a tour around St Andrews, my home town and one of the most haunted in the country, during which we met up with another team member, Kyle Stewart, who was good enough to guide us around the castle. After sharing the tales of witchcraft, religious battles, violent executions and sieges, we headed off along the coast to the Wemyss Caves, via an award winning Fish and Chip shop that turned out not to have award winning burgers. The clue was in the title! The Wemyss Caves are known to have been occupied by humans for over 2000 years, and with such a wealth of history, It is not surprising to learn of a ghost story or 2 connected to them. The caves, along with MacDuff's Castle which sits perched on the clifftop above, have been the focus of an in depth investigation by Scottish Paranormal, where we have explored and uncovered the tale of the best known of these ghosts, Mary Sibbald. It seems the spirit of Mary was curious as to whom the visitor to the caves was, and she came forward to communicate with us, but refused to respond to questions posed by Rick. This would change later in the night.

Our next stop was Balgonie Castle, a hidden gem and home of around 11 ghosts! A warm welcome waited from the Laird of Balgonie Castle, and after showing Rick around, we settled into our evening investigation. By this time, we had been joined by Kyle once again, as well as our team members, Nichola Dignan and Cheryl Meikle. Our research has led us to believe that Mary Sibbald was the daughter of an early Laird of Balgonie, struck from the historical records for falling in love with the leader of a group of local gypsies in the 15th century, and she once again came forward to communicate with us in the Great Hall. This time she was happy to answer questions posed by Rick, responding by triggering the lights on his KII meter. It was an interesting session, with the door rattling and unexplained wheezes also being heard, yet the ghosts of the castle were just warming up.

We headed to the castle's chapel, an area where we have documented a lot of activity during earlier investigations. In the Chapterhouse, the room before the chapel itself, Mary once again made her presence known and was responding to Rick's questions so quickly he had to call on us to give more to ask. Once inside the chapel, Rick caught what looked like a tall, dark shadow of a man standing behind the altar, possibly with wings, on his thermal imaging camera. Little did we realize this was a warning of what was to come? While asking questions, Cheryl at first, and then Ally were drawn to something to the rear of the room. As Ally watched, a hooded figure with no face formed, and then disappeared as quickly when he alerted us to its presence. Kyle went to sit where the figure had appeared, but a crushing headache soon forced him to move to another part of the room.

No other activity occurred in the chapel, but with adrenaline still running high we returned to the Chapterhouse to gather our thoughts, where the castle's spirits would deliver one final piece of evidence to our guest. As we stood and discussed the day's events, Cheryl reacted to a light anomaly she spotted rising from behind Rick. At the exact same moment, he reacted to feeling something hit him on the back of the head! There did not seem to be any malice in this, we see it as a final reminder of just how haunted the castle is, and to encourage Rick to return again when next in Scotland.

The whole team thoroughly enjoyed their time with Rick and thanks him for his company. It was great to watch someone with so much experience work and share their knowledge and we do, very much, hope to do it all again soon.

Rick: I had such a fantastic day with this team, they were so kind to put up with my limping slowly everywhere, if there was a sloping area I could see them walking near me just in case I might go tumbling down the hill! A real world class organization and I am proud to call them friends!

The Scottish Paranormal Team

Kyle is in the front. From left to right, Gregor, Nichola, Jonathan, Ryan and Ally sitting down…

Chapter 32
The Real Mary King's Close

Mandy Fellows, Ally Reid, Janet Rust, Ryan O'Neill, J Craig Miller

For several years now I have been lucky enough to hook up with some of the best ghost hunters in Scotland and England where they have hosted me at several fantastic locations. I was looking for a chance to be able to take them somewhere really cool when my friend J Craig Miller, who was the manager of the Real Mary King's Close attraction in Edinburgh, asked me if I would like to get some people together for a ghost hunt.

Well of course I did! The Real Mary King's Close is one of the most well-known ghost hunting spots in all of Scotland; it is an underground part of the city that dates back hundreds of years.

I called my good friend Brian Harley of Premier Paranormal and invited him and a friend, Anne Marie McManus, as well as Mandy Fellows from Anubis Paranormal in England, who had taken me to the very haunted Bolton Abbey in Yorkshire. She brought along Gary Fields, who had a television show as a psychic medium, as well as Janet Rust, another member of her team to join us.

I then called my friend Gregor Stewart of Scottish Paranormal who had taken me to all the hotspots in St. Andrews and to two caves along the coast as well as the fabulous Balgonie Castle. I had also ghost hunted with Ally Reid and Ryan O'Neill of Scottish Paranormal and also invited them to join the hunt, and unfortunately Gregor couldn't make it but thankfully the other two could.

I met Craig and Cat Mowat, the Retail Duty Manager who also works at the Close ; they would be our guides for the night at the front entrance to the Real Mary King's Close. Craig, Cat and I went over the parameters for that night's hunt while we waited for the others to arrive. We all finally met up at the designated time of 11:00 p.m. and headed into the building.

We were given a quick tour of the close, and then we split up into different teams, we tried to make sure everybody got a chance to ghost hunt with different people from different groups, one of the things I really stressed was paraunity, which thankfully all of them not only agreed to but were very much in favor of.

If you have not seen this venue on television, it is actually built into the side of a Hill which makes most of it underground , And the building itself is made out of that old time stone very similar to what castles are made out of. There is a very magical feel to the Close; there have been many reports of paranormal activity, so we were all excited to get to the hunt. We separated into 2 groups, my group went in to the doll Room, and it is a Room full of toys for children that people from around the world have left for the little spirits to play with. The other group went into another room down the hallway.

We tried to get some evidence in Annie's Room but nothing seemed to come forward, but the room held a very good surprise for us. As we were standing there I was watching the faces of the girls that were with me as well as Ally Reid, because I was hearing something very ominous sounding and I was watching their faces to see if they were hearing it also. As I looked I could see them looking around so I know they were hearing something. So I ask them what they were hearing, and to a person they all said the same thing… What were we all hearing? We were hearing what can be described as nothing other than a heartbeat, what it could possibly be we had no idea.

Where we heard the heartbeat

My group decided to start an investigation in the hallway near us and that is when the K2 meter started to blow up.

Ally and I were getting five light responses to our questions and then suddenly they were gone…

Ryan O'Neill's write up on Mary Kings Close

The Real Mary Kings Close: The depths of Mary Kings Close are no stranger to me due to a plethora of paranormal research I've conducted in this area of Edinburgh. I've written extensively about this in both my upcoming book "The Unseen Worlds" and on my website for people to freely access at Haunted Scotland.

I know the location is haunted, I can truly say this without a shred of doubt and without any need to hype the location or its non-physical inhabitants. When the invite to join Rick McCallum of Hollywood Ghost Hunters came to the Scottish Paranormal team - after an amazing time with Rick the previous week - it was a no-brainer for us. Unfortunately, Greg Stewart could not make this one due to holiday commitments, and I truly wanted Greg to join Ally Reid here so they could soak up the atmosphere. I knew beforehand that physical activity would present itself, no need for ITC Research, EVP work or other high tech here, plainly old school techniques work amazingly at this location.

We arrived on site at 11 pm to be greeted by the collaboration team led by Rick. Being massive on unity and cooperation, Rick managed to bring together a selection of UK teams for the evening, further proving that in this field, we have people with such love for the topic and progression of the subject. We were escorted down to Annie's Room to join up with Rick, Mandy & Janet. Straight away, I was aware of spirit interaction with the team. Various movements on the floor, light bumps, bangs and dragging noises above us. Let's be clear, above our heads was the basements of the city chambers which was locked up, no one is in there and this is the fact of the matter here. This was not some small rodent running around and as I am about to reveal, things were to get even more astonishing for the team.

Rick led the quiet sessions; ensuring noise levels were low and awareness level high. Full concentration as we called out in hushed tones for the unseen energies to continue with the interaction. While this was underway, we tried to locate the sounds and observed the EMF meters fluctuate in a fashion that was not natural in the slightest. At times, I marveled as Rick managed to gain direct interaction via such techniques. It was the next occurrence that would draw our breath such was the blatant action of the activity. As we stood in the hallway between little Annie's room and the cattle shed, we proceeded to be stunned as childlike footsteps ran the length of the corridor we were in, but, above our heads. We double checked exactly what was above us - although I already knew but we must do the checks - with our hosts for the evening. We thought Impossible and pleasantly shocking at the same time. Had we just heard one of the resident spirits of Mary Kings Close? We all heard it, we all stood in wonder and we were all satisfied that we had experienced a real event of the old-school nature.

We would then begin our descent further down the close to Chesney's House. We had mixed results here, we could have had a few direct hits via the KII for sure, and we called for caution though, as it was not 100% spot on interaction. However, as we finished up in this house, we moved out into the close and things again began to get a little strange. We all clearly heard movement, as if the other team were coming towards us. No one appeared though, and we were all left scratching our heads. Door leading to nowhere were heard rattling, handles and bangs evident. Yet, no physical source was present to cause such activity. This was overall as expected, perhaps a little more than usual but certainly up there as one of the best physical wise with pure old-school type investigating. No overly flashy equipment or technology, just pure senses and deep dark underground Edinburgh. Such was the activity early on, I even decided to go with it and not attempt any audio sessions. Why ruin the atmosphere with noise when the unseen inhabitants were letting us know they were clearly with us.

It was an amazing night underground and amazing people to spend it with. I thank Rick greatly for this, an excellent researcher and investigator and genuinely kindhearted guy who we enjoy spending time with.

Chapter 33
Colonel Allensworth State Park

I was very excited to be invited to this charity event that was to benefit a local Animal Shelter, and was looking forward to meeting some new paranormal people, as well as Michelle Wagner and Jamie Menshouse, who I had become friends with at Scarefest in Lexington Kentucky.

I had about a two and a half hour drive to the event, and was expecting to have a good time, but I wasn't expecting much as far as getting any really good paranormal evidence… Man, was I wrong!

I made it to the park and got to the house we would being staying in, it was an older building with a long hallway that had rooms on both sides, and I was shown to my room… that hallway would later provide me with one of the best paranormal experiences in my life, and I would actually discover an ability that I didn't know I had..

Rick McCallum

As we were all gathered and meeting each other, munching on all the snacks in the kitchen, I was sitting with Jamie Menshouse, her lovely daughter Alley, Mikey and Michelle Wagner when we decided to walk to the church, of the places we would be ghost hunting the next day…Mikey, Jamie, Alley and I headed out.

We got to the church and it was locked, but it had a window over the doorway that was too high for any of us to peek in… Alley told us she had been there earlier and stuck her ear to the door and heard something growl. Now that made me very curious because, well, I get growled at occasionally… ok, a lot!

We decided that Mikey, who is a big guy, would get Alley on his shoulders so she could take a picture of the interior of the church. Alley has a professional grade camera, but it was too dark in the church, so I, being vertically enhanced and all, being 6' 4" helps every once in a while, so I turned on the flashlight on my cell phone and standing on my tip toes placed the phone flat on the window.. Alley began snapping away… Mikey lowered her down and we started looking at what she got, and what she got was very compelling… As we all huddled around the camera, the consensus was that what looked to be a large cat, and I mean cougar sized was jumping over the pews! Even more compelling was the fact that we could see through it! What a great start to the hunt.

Alley Rader's picture

Ghosts Believe in Me

We returned to the house where we sat and chatted about Alley's picture when people went outside, leaving myself and Alley at the table... We bonded instantly, I know, what in the world could a 16 year old girl and a beat up old stuntman have in common? It turns out we love ghost hunting, photography, and Alley is an extraordinary photographer, and if she pursues it I have no doubt she will be famous, she really is that good... and weird senses of humor... We chatted about life in general while I was making a valiant effort to eat my own bodyweight in chocolate chip cookies, when she asks me "don't you have Type 2 diabetes?" I said yes and then she just shakes her head and says "keep it up and you'll have Type 1, 2 and 3"...

The other people returned and we all sat around chatting when Alley got me again... she looks over and says "you are in pretty good shape... for a fossil"... How could you not like that sense of humor? Her mom Jamie was getting a kick out of us sparring back and forth, when she called me a fossil everybody looked at me to see how I would respond, but I just cracked up, it was a very good smack down... but that was just the warmup for what was about to occur..

Michelle Wagner, who I knew from Scarefest, and who is a very well-known psychic, suggested we have a Energy Circle, and for those of you who don't know what that is, it is very much like a séance, but you don't try to draw spirits from the other side, you try to communicate with the ones who are already present. We sat at a round table and joined hands, Michelle to my left, Alley to my right, then Jamie and Mikey... Michelle began calling spirits forward and it didn't take long till our equipment started going off, my K2 was responding to us, as the other equipment was also reacting. I had never been in an Energy Circle before so I was just following Michelle's lead, we were all asking questions when all of a sudden I could see the long hallway where are bedrooms were. I saw this in my mind, not with my eyes. I had never had this happen before but I am smart enough to know when something amazing is happening… I could not see the hallway from where I was, but it was clear as a bell, like watching a black and white TV. I told them there was a man standing at the end of the hallway by the window… as I was speaking he started moving forward and I started telling everyone what I was seeing, I told them it was a tall white man with a bald head, which was interesting because the house and all of the buildings were built and had been occupied by African Americans… The man stopped just before the doorway, I could see just inside the door but he didn't come far enough for me to see him with my eyes… all of I sudden I heard his voice very clearly say "I'm gone"… No one else heard it, but I insisted that he said it, so Mikey checked the voice recorder and as he did you can clearly hear a voice say "I'm gone", and a few seconds later me saying I heard him… and then he was gone! As we kept going with the circle, I was suddenly hit with what seemed like a shot of electricity, strong enough to make my upper body shake.. I don't know why it happened, but I suspect the energy was a culmination of the energy, and most certainly the strongest energy came from Michelle Wagner, and I suspect she probably provided the energy for me to be able to see the man in the hallway.

Michelle said there was another energy showing up, and I could also see it but it wasn't shaped like a person, it was a dark shadow at the spot the other one had just left. I had an overwhelming feeling this was an evil entity, as did Michelle. Michelle and I were facing the doorway, Mikey, Jamie and Alley had their backs to it..

Michelle was talking to the shadow trying to get it to show itself when I seemed to be able to understand what it was up to, Mikey was feeling the presence behind him, Jamie seemed to be aware of it also.. it was right at this point that I heard, not like the "I'm gone" from earlier but as if I picked up on the entity's intent… it instantly pissed me off, so I told everybody that the entity had its sight set on one particular person. I wanted to see if more was being sent my way when it seemed as if the entity was getting stronger. Mikey asked me who it was after, but I didn't want to scare anyone so I just said let's try to get rid of it… Mikey wanted to know, I think he wanted to help scare it off, but wanted to know who it was focused on… I looked at Michelle and said it is after Alley… Well that got the party started! Jamie instantly turned into Mama Grizzly and told it in no uncertain terms that it was not going to get anywhere near her daughter! I then said" I know what you are, and I will not let you near her, we will not let you near her so you are ordered to leave… Michelle then told it to leave and in just a moment the feeling of the presence was gone… I think our combined strength scared it off…

I truly think that Michelle Wagner has amazingly strong psychic ability, and I have always felt the spirits, so I think that I could actually see and hear them was probably jumpstarted by holding her hand, and the power from the Energy Circle.

Very happy to say that the ghost hunt was very well attended, and a hockey mask that Kane had autographed made a couple of hundred dollars for the animal shelter!

Alley Rader, Jamie Menshouse, and Michelle Wagner

The Strange Case of Donna

I had gotten a call from a very nice lady, a real sweetheart named Donna, who told me her house was haunted and she thought something was trying to attach itself to her. We made a time for me to investigate, and I grabbed my friend Louis Horowitz to go with me. Louis is also a member of my team.

When we arrived we were greeted by Donna, a very sweet African American woman, she had that bubbly kind of personality that you instantly like. She showed us around her apartment, a two story loft.

We stopped and chatted, listened to her tell of occurrences, and hot spots, then we had her stay down stairs while we went through the place. It had a very quiet vibe to the place, and none of our equipment went off, there was no feeling of a spirit presence at all, so we headed back down, where I told Donna that there was no evidence that her apartment was haunted. Her reply stunned me... "Oh, I don't think it's haunted either" she said. "WHAT"? Then why the heck did you call me? is what I was thinking. Before I can say anything, Donna quietly tells me she thinks something is attaching itself to her, that she feels changes in her health and personality. I know I need to help her, maybe if I check her over with some equipment and show her there is nothing there that she will feel better.

I took out my K2 meter, ran it all around her without any response. I decided to film her with my night vision camera. Again, there was nothing. I am hoping she is feeling better by my not finding anything when I have an inspiration. I have recently started using a FLIR for Android thermal imager, and have had good results with it, so I'm sure when I show her the recording and there is nothing there that maybe she will feel better that there is no evidence of an attachment. I almost fell over when I looked at the screen! On the right side of her stomach was a black spot, roughly six inches by four inches. The human form is very warm, 98.6 degrees is normal, and a person will be a very bright image of white, yellow and orange. The spot was very cold. It also was very dark, a kind of purplish black, showing it to be much, much colder than the rest of her.

I stood there for a moment, pondering the possibilities, and began asking her questions. Is there anything under her shirt where the spot is, a cell phone, a belt buckle, anything? I had her turn in a circle to make sure it wasn't a camera anomaly. Nope, still there! I had her walk up to the second floor and walk back down, still there.

I showed her the pictures, and she gets extremely excited. I calm her down and tell her if I were her I would see a doctor as soon as possible, as this might be a blockage of some kind, or some other medical issue.

She asks me if it is an attachment what she can do to get rid of it. I explain that anything I tell her is just conjecture, but I know people have had success by firmly telling it to leave.

Is it ok if I use my faith to help she asks? I reply that I certainly don't think it could hurt, but to be very firm and ORDER it to leave. I was not expecting what happened next...Donna launched into a verbal attack and calling on her faith like a revival minister and told it to leave and never come back. The level of intensity was awesome; I wish I had filmed it! I know it is trendy to call women fierce, but there is no other way to describe it! She was yelling "get out! Get out!" She was so convincing I almost left! I waited for a few minutes while she cooled down, then I scanned her again with the thermal.

There was nothing there...

Chapter 34
England is Extraordinarily Haunted

I had been in a car for about five hours as Brian Harley of Premier Paranormal, Carol Ann Hosburgh and I were driving from Edinburgh to Liverpool, England to meet up with Garry Fields, who was kind enough to be putting us up for the night after our investigations.

We were going to investigate Bolton Abbey, but first we went to Norwich Theatre, and here is Mandy Fellows of Anubis Paranormal Investigators take on what happened…

> While on location at the Northwich Plaza I was carrying out a paranormal investigation with some great friends of mine, Rick being one of them.
>
> We decided to head off down to the cellar of the old theatre which was now an old disused bingo hall, I, Rick, Brian Harley and Dave Hart wandered down the steps into the dark, and we walked around for a minute or two and had a look with the torches at what was around us. We had a barrier in front of us which halved the cellar, Dave turned on the PSB11 (Spirit Box) and we listened for a while, and then went dark to heighten our senses.
>
> Brian was to the right of us looking under the stage and Dave was also to the right. We listened to the box for a while and we were getting a males voice through, we didn't really get a name or anything that we could make sense of just that is was a male. We

had limited light from the trap door above us which we had come down, and as we were going to go back up I spotted a man the other side of the barrier about 4 ft. in front of me and Rick.

The man was looking down, quite possibly into his hands or at something on the floor, I looked for a minute as I knew Dave and Brian had not crossed the barrier or left the right side of me. I turned to look at Rick who was to the left of me as he turned to look at me and at the same time we both said "you did see that right" and then we looked back but the man was gone. It was such an amazing experience and I was so glad Rick had seen it too, as Dave and Brian hadn't, and we both had so it was good that it was seen by two independent witnesses.

We waited for a bit longer to see if he would appear again but sadly he never returned, but we thanked spirit for showing themselves to us as I felt so privileged to see it and we went back up the wooden stairs to recall our experience to the rest of the folk who were investigating with us xx

I was standing right next to the barrier that separated the room, there were electric boxes, and things for the theatre along the far wall, leaving an open space probably eight to ten feet from the wall, that area was wide open. I was looking at my K2 meter when I looked up and there was a man standing in the dark not more than four feet from me. I initially thought one our group had crossed the barrier that is how clear the apparition was, so that I turned to see which one it might be, as everybody was slightly behind me and to my right. Surprise! Everybody was on our side of the barrier.

It was only roughly five seconds since I had seen the apparition, so I quickly turned back toward it, but it was gone. Thankfully, Mandy had also seen him… The other people also had experiences, Brian Harley in particular who saw an elderly lady, not once but twice, I believe Carol Ann also saw it…

I met some very nice people there, including Emma Firth and Dave Hart of Forgotten Era Paranormal; they really took the time to show me the whole theatre! Norwich Theatre turned out spectacular!

Bolton Abbey, Yorkshire, England

As we approached Bolton Abbey I was struck by the raw beauty of such an ancient place, and was very excited to ghost hunt the Priory, as you have to have special permission, as there is a bailiff who keeps an eye out, but we were lucky that Brian Harley had a contact who granted us access.

There is so much paranormal activity at Bolton Abbey it is hard to process all that went on there. It is a beautiful place, there were people walking around enjoying the nice sunny day… and then the night came and everything changed…

As soon as we drove up to Bolton Abbey, I could feel the energy, it felt like it was simmering, just waiting for us to enter the grounds. Brian Harley had lived near here and had been to Bolton many times and really wanted to come back to check it out again.

We all split up into small groups, and Carol Ann and I were checking out different spots, just going where our instincts took us, and at one time we were standing looking into the chapel when we both saw a dark figure standing about ten yards away, next to the corner of the chapel. We turned toward it and it darted behind the building, it had been right next to the corner, so it only had to move a few feet before it disappeared behind the chapel. Carol Ann and I immediately took off around the corner, but the figure was gone. That however would not be the last dark shadow we would encounter that night.

Mandy Fellows of Anubis Paranormal Investigators is also a psychic medium, and during the evening she felt drawn to the creek behind the chapel, and she saw a figure heading from the creek towards the chapel, I wonder if it was the same one we saw, but I think they were different because of what happened next…

Where Mandy Fellows saw the dark figure

I had been standing off in this one area about fifty yards from the opening you go through to reach the chapel. Carol Ann had gone to check on something, and I saw her coming towards me. She got about five yards from me and suddenly looked startled. She asked me how long I had been investigating there, and I replied about fifteen minutes. Now anyone who knows me knows that I almost always wear all black clothes, so what Carol Ann said next made sense. She said she was coming from the chapel and saw a big black shape in front of her, and it being dark anyway she followed it thinking it was me, but when she saw me ahead of her she realized it wasn't me she was following… That is three dark shapes that we had seen… very interesting.

The Abbey had more surprises in store for us, something that I found very compelling. There is a story of the Abbey that the spirits won't let you leave if they have targeted you, and it always happens near the exit gate, which is about a ten foot wide gateway... As Mandy approached the gate, followed by Carol Ann and myself, we saw the chain she was wearing, she had gotten it from the Vatican, get yanked, leaving a burn mark on her neck from the chain where was pulled. We were standing a few feet from the gate, when Mandy told us about the spirits trying to keep people from going through the gate and keeping them on the grounds. Now, what you have to know about Mandy and Carol Ann is that neither of them are the timid type, so when Mandy said she felt something trying to keep her from leaving I knew it wouldn't be able to stop her and she went through, then Carol Ann said she felt the energy as well, but she too made it through. I walked through without feeling anything. (Maybe it wanted me to leave?)

It was so odd and out of character for both them, they are both excellent and seasoned paranormal investigators, so I knew that something strange was going on near that gate, and decided to keep my eyes open when others would get there.

Bolton Abbey

It was also the night I was introduced to midgies, these vicious little bugs that swarm your face… I slapped my face so many times it felt raw. Horrible little buggers… My face hadn't been slapped that many times since the last time I went to a country bar…

Garry Fields, Carol Ann, Mandy, Eddie Fellows, Gary Hughill and Brian Harley were standing on the altar area; the altar itself had been gone for at least one hundred years I would guess. The altar had been the site of witchcraft and evil rituals, not by the Abbey, but by groups who had snuck in.

I was with two bouncers from Liverpool, Justin Lee and Peter Monkman, who had come along as well, and we were on the outside of the Abbey when we heard a loud commotion coming from inside, so we hurried around the corner to see what was happening, and were surprised to see Brian flat on his back, totally out of it. The group told us they had seen something come towards them very fast, then one of them said when they turned to see Brian, he was last in line, they described his movement as being on roller skates, and then he went down. We got him out of the Abbey and we watched over him till he came around… He was shivering, and we had put our coats on him to warm him up, when he said he was feeling a bit better… A couple people went to get the truck so they could take him to base camp and get some coffee in him to warm him up.

Now I want to say that I totally trust the word of all these people, they are all very experienced investigators, and when they told me what had happened I believed them, I had never seen anyone go out like that before, but you should have seen how they all jumped into action to help Brian!

Peter and I, he was one of the bouncers, grabbed Brian under the arms and steadied him so he could get to the truck. We basically half carried him under the arms and as we approached the gate I watched carefully to see if Brian would feel the same energy that Mandy and Carol Ann had when they tried to go through the gate.

Brian was still half out of it, he had his head down as Peter and I were moving him forward, I know by how he was looking at the ground that he couldn't possibly see the gate.

We got about ten feet from the gate when Brian's head popped up, and he started shoving backwards, like he was trying not to leave.

Peter and I are both pretty big guys and we lifted him up under the arms and took him through the gate, got him in the truck where they took him to base camp, where he finally started to feel like himself again. I found it very compelling that he had reacted to the gate the way he did, when I know he couldn't see it... It was very interesting for sure.

Bolton Abbey was a real treat, and in my opinion there are a lot a strange things there, the dark figures, the aggressiveness that affected Brian, the mysterious energy near the gate all make me wonder if the witchcraft and Satanic rituals didn't call something forward...

We packed up, jumped into our cars for the drive home, we were in Garry Fields car, a really nice BMW, I was in the front passenger seat, I couldn't fit in the back, and Carol Ann and Brian were in the back seat. What happened next will always be with me...

It is very late, and there is hardly any traffic on the highway, when suddenly Carol Ann cries out "what the bloody hell!"

As soon as she yells, the car goes hard left, and I can see there are no cars around us, so I thought Garry had fallen asleep so I turned to grab the wheel, and as I was turning I could hear him saying " not today, not today, prayers and light, prayers and light".

Now I am totally confused, there is no other traffic for him to have taken such a hard evasive turn. Little did I know that he may just have saved our lives! Because I am tall, the roof blocked my vision of anything up high, and what had happened was that Garry and Carol Ann had both seen a young guy perched on the OUTSIDE of the overpass, his hands were behind him hanging on, and when he saw us coming in the lane below him, he crouched to jump and to commit suicide. If they hadn't seen him, and if Garry didn't react as quickly and as well as he did, that guy may have landed on the car, which appeared to be his intent. Because Garry had swerved left, the guy didn't jump…

Garry called the police, and there is a totally different dynamic in England when it comes to 911 calls. Garry tells her about the guy on the bridge, she replies Bridge 31, and they are already on their way love, thank you for calling darling…

We found the next day that Mandy and her group, who were way behind us, had seen the police pulling him up to safety, thank goodness. And speaking of thanking people this one is for Garry Fields, thank you, well done mate!

Chapter 35
The Hell Fire Club

I couldn't help but be very anxious as we approached the Hell Fire Club in Dublin, Ireland.

The Hell Fire Club is reputed to be one of the most haunted locations in all of Ireland and as we all hopped out of the car it was then that I realized this might be a bit harder than Old Rick had anticipated!

The Club is at the top of a steep hill, and a VERY long walk uphill. As you know I need knee replacement surgery on my right knee from a really hard fall I took in Rosslyn Forest. It had been raining, so the trails were muddy, and as I had hurt my knee on a muddy hill, I was afraid I wouldn't be able to make it. We all started out, and I was determined to make it even if I had to drag myself.

I didn't fly from the US to Scotland, then to Belfast, then a long drive to Dublin to wait in the car. The team split up, most going up the trails, but fortunately there was a gravel road that Greg Stewart, Johnathan Garaway and I took to get up the hill. It was a lot farther than the trails, so I knew the guys went with me so I wouldn't have to go alone. Pretty good guys if you ask me! I would guess it took at least a half hour to get to the top, but just as we crested the hill, there it was. It was a very old all stone building, with a forest behind it, the tree line was very dark and ominous, and I couldn't help but feel that would be a hot spot if we ever came back, but todays hunt was for the building itself.

The stonework was amazing, we toured the place to get our bearings, and then we split up to get the hunt started. I was going from group to group, see what kind of activity they were getting, mostly just small stuff, but we had just gotten there, I knew it would start to heat up. And it certainly didn't disappoint!

> Having visited other locations connected to the Hellfire Club, such as Gilmerton Coves in Edinburgh, the trip to their base on Montpelier Hill in Ireland had been one I had wanted to make for some time. And what better way to do it that with team mates and good friends, Ryan, Ally, Kyle and Jonathan, group members Eileen and Tommy and off course our special guest and our friend, Rick.
>
> The first observation I made was Montpelier Hill is big and steep! While I took the much longer, but gentler path round and up with Jonathan and Rick, the others shot off up the hill into the mist like mountain goats. While the sensible path may have been longer, it did take you through the forest around the hill, where it is believed many dark ceremonies have taken place and it certainly did have an atmosphere, one that was to be experienced by the rest on the way back down.
>
> When we reached the building a second observation hit me, just how high and remote we were. It makes you wonder why anyone

would want to create a clubhouse in a location so difficult to access, which only fuels the thoughts about what exactly the members of the Hellfire Club were getting up to there. At least they didn't have to bring the building material far; it is believed that the stones from ancient burial chambers on the hill were used in the construction, which only adds to reasons for paranormal activity at the location.

The whole site had an energy that you could sense, there was a feeling of being watched from the woodland when outside and the dark rooms of the building itself only added to the eerie feeling. One room, half way up the stairs to the rear was particularly dark and felt quite foreboding. On the top floor, overlooking the city of Dublin, we watched as Rick carried out a session with his K2 EMF meter. We have watched Rick use this method before, and he had a good connection to spirit through this device. Sure enough, he was soon getting direct reactions to the questions he was asking through the lights on the meter illuminating. Of particular interest was Rick is a descendent of John Wilkes, a prominent member of the Hellfire Club who is famed for releasing a baboon into the club's premises in High Wycombe, England, in the late 1700s. Rick seemed to establish a direct connection with his relative, and to validate this when we switched to use an audio device, when asking to confirmation of what had happened the broken but clear word 'Ba………Boon' came through.

After we finished our investigation, everyone decided to take the long path back due it starting to rain and being dark, making the hillside quite dangerous. The feeling of being watched intensified as we made our way back, and evidence of rituals were spotted in the woods. In my opinion this location certainly lived up to expectations, and that experience was only enhanced by having a decedent of a well-known member of the original club with us. Gregor Stewart

I walked into another room where Ally Reid was using a voice recorder, I had my K2 meter. We started asking questions, and we started getting intelligent responses on the meter, very strong responses, four and five light responses. We continued on for about five to ten minutes, then boom, it was gone…

Kyle Stewart was in another room, and had a very strong connection working; here is his remembrance of the club…

I had the pleasure of joining Rick McCallum on a trip to Ireland. When we got to Ireland we went to the Hell Fire Club near Dublin and it was quite a climb to get to the top. Once we got to the top the views despite being slightly cloudy were absolutely fantastic and the Club itself was a magnificent building.

We conducted an investigation within the Hell Fire Club and I was very pleased to have Rick with me at the time as he had relatives that were senior members of the Hell Fire Club when it was still in use. We got very intelligent responses and felt we were in touch with Rick's relative. I then went into a room by myself at the back of the Club. I felt sadness in the room and guilt as if I have done something wrong. I then discovered that I had potentially connected with a spirit who I believed to be called Martin. He claimed to me he felt guilt for what he did in the club and wanted closure. Not even a minute or so later I felt at ease in the pressure of the room and felt it becoming more open. I felt another connection was coming through and this was of a woman called Michelle. I feel Martin had regrettably done things to Michelle and wanted closure and when she came through I felt forgiveness. Just as the pressure of Michelle giving Martin forgiveness lifted, the room's atmosphere changed to a more calming feeling and a feather flew through the door and landed right at my feet. Was this a sign of them saying thank you to me for helping them out?

I then told Rick and the team and they were amazed and said to keep the feather. I kept the feather throughout my whole trip to Ireland. Rick had asked me as I am an amateur photographer if I could take a photo of him looking out the window overlooking the city of Dublin. I was excited to do so as I wanted to capture the building itself and the view of Dublin but also show how passionate Rick is in this field. I was very happy with the results and Rick was over the moon! Rick had a K2 meter which measures electromagnetic energy in the air and he communicated to different energies very well and professionally. It was very impressive and I was glad to be part of this experience. Throughout the time at the Hell Fire Club it was great to see how respectful Rick was of spirit residing there and I feel through being respectful and respected by spirit he got very relevant and timely responses.

Johnathan Garaway, Gregor Stewart, Eileen Murray, Ryan O'Neill, Kyle Stewart

Eileen Murray

> On the afternoon of Saturday 31st March 2019, I was in the company of Rick McCallum investigating the Hell Fire Club county Dublin, Ireland with Scottish Paranormal. We were using a spirit box and Rick was calling out for a relative of his, John Wilkes, who had been a member of this club. After a few minutes, and clear as day, "Hi Rick" came through, followed a short time later by "relative". Rick then started to question if it was true that this relation of his had released a baboon into the club, as is anecdotally thought to have occurred, when "baboon" was heard. Unfortunately we did not have a recorder running at the time, which is a great pity as it was very clear, and an intelligent response to the questions Rick was asking at the time. I am happy to validate this experience.

When I first discovered that John Wilkes was a relative, and had been a Member of Parliament and also had held many other high ranking positions, and had also turned a baboon dressed like Satan loose I checked him out, and was excited when I read that he was considered the most charming man in England… I was thinking "yeah, the most charming man, that's my relative", all proud … until I read the next line… "He had to be charming, for he was also by far the ugliest"…

Leap Castle, Ireland

As I sit here to write this, I'm very conflicted, trying to decide whether to tell the story or not, because what happened to me was so intense that I felt that no one would believe it. I hardly believe it myself…

Ghosts Believe in Me

I decided it needed to go in the book as a strong warning that ghost hunting can have some very severe complications. I have included an eyewitness account from a very accomplished paranormal investigator about what he saw, and at any place in this book you may wonder about, if there were other people there I put in what they saw as well.

The picture Kyle took of me is the cover of this book

Many of you know me, and if you don't, then I must really stress that my name and integrity are the most important things to me, and this story is as close to being exact as I can make it.

We had just made the long climb down the mountain from the Hell Fire Club, just as darkness was falling. It was very eerie walking through the forest in that light, but I really enjoyed the scenery, and Eileen Murray was nice enough to go the long way on the gravel road with me, I knew my knee would not fare well if I slipped in the mud.

We headed towards the Castle, about an hour away. Sitting in the passenger seat, with Ally driving and Ryan and Gregor in the back, we were all having a great time, Ryan was cracking me up with his antics, and I was having a great time.

I started to get a small headache behind my eye, but that didn't bother much, it wasn't very painful. I closed my eyes and sat back in my seat, listening to the guys. It was right about then that I started to get a very strong feeling of apprehension and told Ally. I started to feel worse; my head was swimming a little so I sat there quietly.

Once again I had a bad feeling about Leap Castle, and I have never had that type of feeling before, and if you know me at all you know that won't stop me. I mean, if I'm not afraid of being thrown off roofs or off the hoods of speeding cars, you can bet I'm not going to be afraid of a castle. On the other hand I have learned to trust my instincts so I was wondering what might be giving me these warning signals.

Down this long dark country road we went and there was the castle on the right. It looked awesome! We were early so we parked on the road in front of the castle. It was a great sight, we were next to stone walls on each side of the road, and it was a classic looking Irish country back road, and as we stepped into the darkness, it was cold and windy, and it felt good and I was glad to get out of the car and stretch my legs… The other guys got back in the car where it was warm, I'm not sure about Ally, but I didn't see anyone by the car. Then it started, unquestionably the most intense experience of my life.

Suddenly, and this is exactly the way I described it that night, is that I felt like spear went through my right eye, I could actually feel it going through! The pain was horrendous, my knees buckled, and I was struggling to stay on my feet, but I was losing the battle. I staggered backwards across the street and was fighting regain my balance, my eye was gushing water and I had my hand over it, and somewhere deep down I knew something very serious was going on, and that if I hit the ground, my instincts told me I would never get up. I was able to stagger back towards the car. I heard someone calling my name; it seemed so far away,

I was very nearly unconscious… I heard my name again and saw Ally coming towards me and he helped to the trunk of the car. He grabbed some water and I drank a bit of it. He tried to get me to get back in the car, but I was still very dazed and wanted to stay in the cold air, I thought that might help. I saw Ally get back in the car.

It got worse... my head was swimming, and I couldn't catch my breath, so I grabbed onto the car to keep myself up, but kind of slumped against it. I couldn't breathe, I was trying as hard as I could to suck in some air but it wasn't working...

I was fighting as hard as I could to breathe, and not to fall to the ground. I was almost completely out, my vision was narrowing and I was positive that I was dying... Ally grabbed me and put me in the car...

Ally Reid remembers

We then hit the road as we still had around an hour drive before Leap Castle. A quick petrol and coffee stop! Rick was on good form! He was his usual joking self and winding us all up. The drive passed quickly as we hit the country road for the castle the feelings changed and the excitement grew! We had been discussing the Hell Fire Club but that quickly dried up for the time being as the energy shifted around us all. Having investigated with Rick on several occasion and knowing him closely, he has never showed any signs of fear or feelings prior to a location or investigation. I was driving he turned and looked at me and said he felt real apprehensive. He had a sore head and eye effectively an eye headache if that makes sense. He then said he felt like he was being affected by something. We perhaps at the time did not take it as seriously as we should have. He said he had a funny feeling about Leap and that he wasn't feeling great.

We arrived at the castle a little earlier than planned so decided to park outside the main castle gates. We all jumped out for some fresh air and a much needed toilet break. It was cold and dark! We were in the middle of the Irish countryside the wind was picking up and blowing a shivering cold blast. Greg and Ryan had already jumped back in the car to stay warm.

I turned around and looked back at Rick and I saw him stumble across the road almost like he had lost his balance. I called for him a few times! RICK! Rick, nothing it was on the third occasion he eventually mumbled back to me yeah I'm ok! I knew he wasn't! I got him over to the wall by the car he seemed extremely zoned out by this's time he was then looking in the back of the car for … well I actually don't know! I told him to get back in the car but he said he wanted to get some air for a moment or two!

I gave him some water and made sure he was safe and secure away from any potential traffic. I got back in the car and said guys we have a real problem here! Both Greg and Ryan looked at me in suspense, they knew something was not right, the color drained from them, and I said Rick is not right.

They had already picked up on the vibes as to what was happening. Greg said he had seen him stumble prior to me witnessing him doing it again later. I looked out the side mirror and could just make Rick out leaning down beside the car, white as a ghost! Breathing deeply I could see the thrusts and how much he was struggling. I didn't say this to Rick at the time but I said to the guys what are we doing here? I thought in all seriousness that he was going to pass out and possibly not wake up. It was this point I ordered him back into the car.

We entered the castle grounds and drove up to the door. At this point Greg said where's that guy gone? I said what guy the guy? He said the one who just walked past the car? Nobody was there.

As we moved all our gear into the castle Rick asked to just sit in the car for five minutes! This made me worried as this was the golden acorn of the trip. He was in Ireland at Leap Castle and about to meet the Laird, a chance Rick is always gracious for.

He couldn't move, he said just go and set up in the castle, I'll be fine. During all this he never once said he was ill. He is a very stubborn person in this case, so much care for everyone else but never says a word in his own welfare. We personally felt he was deteriorating faster and worse than he was letting on, so we tried to persuade him to come inside to the warmth of the fire and the century old castle, but he would not budge. I said to the Laird of Leap Castle we might need an ambulance on standby, Rick is not well. I gave him more water and kept checking on him, he was sitting there motionless. All that was on my mind was we are going to lose him.

It might all sound dramatic but in all honesty I thought he was on his way out. About 45 mins had passed by now he was slowly starting to talk a bit more as he asked who was walking around the car a second ago. I said no one Rick; we are all locked inside and doubt anyone else would be around! Some will say this could have been hallucinations but I knew it wasn't because Rick was perking up. I eventually got him inside, and he was still white as a sheet but seemed to have focus and attention back. He sat beside the roaring fire in the Lairds chair (it's about the only one he fitted perfectly as it was the biggest) before long he had his trusted K2 meter out and was ready for investigating. I said I don't think you are up for this, you just get comfortable. He said like hell I will, I didn't come to Ireland to just sit here. I knew he was getting back on track!

A couple of hours investigating and it was time to rest up and settle down try grab some sleep. Rick decided to sleep sitting on a chair with a blanket over his head! We knew Rick was back with us at this point, only he would do this! A quick Irish breakfast and it was on the road home again! It wasn't until a week or so later we spoke about what happened and it was at this point we learned a couple of the other guys had experienced similar to Rick, but only the sore eye and head. It was then we realized that we believed a spirit had put their emotion and feelings onto us.

Turns out someone had had a duel back in the day at the Hell Fire Club and had been shot through the eye! It all started to make more sense now. Whatever happened that night I seriously thought we had lost Rick and what the hell where we going to do? I ain't one for possessions but I do believe that night Rick was a victim of something not earth worthy! An experience I'll never forget, not for the great fun we all had but the seriousness of what happened and the dangers of the paranormal. It is not only old unsafe buildings but spirit contact at its most dangerous. This did not last for just a few days either it took a good few weeks and much weight loss before Rick truly bounced back. He had it bad and the mark was left on us all.

The group had gone into the castle, and I stayed still, I was still feeling light headed, when I started losing focus, and it was slowly getting worse to the point I was very close to blacking out, and I remember saying to myself that I think this it, I felt my energy being drained away and finally realized on was on the border of never waking up, but I was fighting it hard as I could, but my energy was almost zero, my vision was waning, when I said out loud " if this is it, I've had a good life, only a few regrets, and I'm OK with it". A very serene feeling came over me, I had no fear at all, and I seemed to relax…

Very shortly I noticed my breathing was more even, so I opened my eyes and saw Ryan peeking in the window, obviously checking up on me, they were pretty concerned because when I would hear a noise by the car I would open my left eye, my right one I kept shut because it stopped watering and I didn't want it to start again, and I had seen different people looking in. I knew I was in good hands.

I was starting to get my strength back when I heard someone else walking on the gravel outside the car. I sat up and looked, and there was no one there! It made me think of the guy Ryan had seen go by in the same spot. Ally came up to the window, I smiled at him and he helped me out of the car and back inside, where I started to feel like myself again. I know some of you will think I am being melodramatic, or overselling the story, but the truth be known is that I held a few things back, some things that are not meant to be shared…

I went on to hunt the castle… but I knew my life changed that night… what happened? I have no idea…

I had gone up to the Bloody Chapel with Eileen Murray and Tommy Moyes and took some pictures; it was a very dark ominous place with an ominous feeling to it.

Here is Eileen Murray's story…

In March 2019 I was part of an investigation team, Scottish Paranormal, at Leap Castle in Ireland; Rick McCallum was in attendance as a guest investigator.

The castle had been occupied for many many years by the O'Carroll Family. Legend has it that one of the family was a priest, he was in the process of saying a mass in the family chapel within the castle, when his brother arrived, he took offence that mass had started without him and he slaughtered the said priest on the spot. The chapel is known nowadays as "The Bloody Chapel".

Within the chapel is also an oubliette where unfortunates were tossed and left to die, some years ago several cart loads of bones were removed during renovations. During our investigation Rick and I spent some time in the chapel, it was in complete darkness, shuffling sounds and movement had been perceived by another team member earlier in the evening. Whilst there I started to call out for Father O'Carroll to come forward, Rick took photographs which, upon inspection later, showed quite dense swirling mists around me as I stood in one corner in close proximity to the oubliette. There was a sense of foreboding and a presence at the time, the photographic evidence confirming these feelings. Rick is an experienced investigator and his camera equipment cannot be questioned... was this Father O'Carroll? A magnificent place with an interesting if somewhat violent history... Worthy of further investigation which I hope to do some time.

I finally got to meet the Laird of the castle in the morning at breakfast, where he serenaded us on a musical instrument called a whistle, and he was extraordinary! We said our goodbyes and back to Scotland!

Exactly what happened to me that night I'll never know...

Now you may be thinking that such an intense occurrence would scare me away from investigating the paranormal, but it had just the opposite effect! I have been looking for practically my whole life for something so strong to prove to me the spirits were there, and as you can see in the book I have had several very memorable experiences, but nothing comes close to the Leap Castle one.

I plan to keep right on chasing ghosts, spirits and seeking out the unexplainable… Heck, I might even write another book! And I am going to name it "My Guardian Angel Just Called for Backup"!

If you have a good story, interview request or any other things, my contact is rick4spirits@aol.com

Notable Places We Have Investigated

Leap Castle (Ireland)

Hell Fire Club (Ireland)

Mansfield Prison

Clive Barker House

Whaley House

Birdcage Theater

Greyfriars Cemetery (Edinburgh)

Trans Allegheny

The Queen Mary

Pioneer Saloon

The Stanley Hotel

Sloss Furnaces

The Real Mary King's Close (Edinburgh)

Bachelors Grove

Old South Pittsburgh Hospital

Linda Vista Hospital

William Heath Davis Museum

Buffalo Central Rail Station

St. Andrews Castle (Scotland)

Battle of Rosslyn 1303 Battlefield

The Oman House

William Wallace Cave (Scotland)

Wemyss Caves (Scotland)

The Pico House (Ghost Adventures)

Palomino Strip Club

Graber Olive House

Gunfight at OK Corral

Dundrum Castle (Ireland)

Balgonie Castle (Scotland

The Pasadena Suicide Bridge

Rosslyn Chapel

Bolton Abbey (England)

Dracula's Castle

Norwich Theater (England)

St. Charles Hotel (New Orleans)

Egyptian Theater

Star of India Ship

Occidental Studios

Southbridge Vaults (Edinburgh)

Hailes Castle (Edinburgh)

Fort Mac Arthur, the Battle of Los Angeles

Made in the USA
Monee, IL
08 April 2025